A Traveller's Guide to

Saudi Arabia

Siân Pritchard-Jones & Bob Gibbons

ISBN: 9798622785788

First edition: January 2020

Second edition: March 2020

Published by:	Expedition World Ltd.
	email: sianpj@hotmail.com
	www.expeditionworld.com
Text & photos:	Siân Pritchard-Jones and Bob Gibbons
	except where credited
Maps:	Bob Gibbons
Cover layout:	Siân Pritchard-Jones and Bob Gibbons
Cover photo:	Rijal al-Ma village
Back cover:	Mada'in Salih
	Old mud mosque, Shaqra
Title page:	Wadi Qaraqir canyon

A Traveller's Guide to
Saudi Arabia

Siân Pritchard-Jones & Bob Gibbons

Government travel advice

You are strongly urged to consult the various government websites for the current advice regarding travel to Saudi Arabia. A few areas of the country are considered a risk. Most of the country is deemed safe, but a few border areas are listed as being 'only for essential travel'. Areas very close to the southern border with Yemen are considered off-limits to travellers.

The emergency number for help on the road and elsewhere is **997.**

Excellent roads cut across the country: route to Al Ula

Warning

Please remember that journeying in remoter areas can be potentially dangerous. The publisher and authors have taken every care in producing this guide, but readers must take ultimate responsibility for themselves. Routes and weather conditions can change suddenly, even volcanoes can erupt! Readers must understand these natural risks. Political issues can occur and readers should keep up to date with any changes.

The authors cannot accept liability for damage of any nature (including damage to property, personal injury or death) arising from the information in this book, directly or indirectly.

Health facilities in the region are generally good. Take a supply of personal medicines you are likely to use, as well as some you do not expect to need. As in many parts of the world, be prepared to help yourself in any eventuality.

Jebel Qidr in the White and Black volcano area

It's a dangerous business, Frodo, going out your door. You step on to the road, and if you don't keep your feet, there's no knowing where you might be swept off to.
The Lord of the Rings, **J R R Tolkien**

About this guide

As Saudi Arabia opens for tourism, it seems appropriate that a special note needs to be added here. We came to Saudi Arabia out of a pure desire to explore, to discover a place that has held so much fascination for so long. It is a country that adventurous travellers will want to experience for themselves; a place that has been off the map for as long as we can remember.

Perhaps it is with a certain arrogance that we want to share a country here that is not ours. We apologise for this. All we can do as outsiders is to provide information so that others, who have the same sense of adventure, can enjoy such a new and exciting destination.

Nobody asked us to write this introductory guide, and it has not been sponsored by anyone.

Whether a visitor seeks to discover the geography, the culture, the people or the history, all aspects of the country will be enlightening. Whatever anyone does decide, there is no doubt that Saudi Arabia is an amazing and surprising place to visit.

Sian and Bob

Enjoying the antiquities: Makkah Gate in Jeddah

Acknowledgements

Thanks to Florent Egal for his help before our trip and for all his amazing efforts to produce a great, informative and inspirational website. See www.saudiarabiatourismguide.com

Special thanks to Axel Michaelowa from Switzerland for his enthusiasm and for the background literature he has collated from many sources.

Many thanks to Mohammad Al-Anazi (Executive Director of Al Ula Cooperative Tourism Association and official licensed tour guide) for organising our 4x4 trip to Jibal al-Rukkab and for always being there on WhatsApp when we had a question about the rest of the country.

Thanks also to the following bloggers:
Joan Torres from Spain: www.againstthecompass.com
Laura Alho: www.blueabaya.com
Susie Johnson Khalil: https://susiesbigadventure.blogspot.com/
and https://susieofarabia.blogspot.com/

Thanks to all at the Red Sea Hotel in Jeddah for a superb start and end to the first trip. To the staff of Enterprise car hire in Jeddah/Riyadh airports for excellent service. Thanks to all the welcoming and hospitable local people who helped us in the streets, at the hotels, the fuel stations and at the sights. For initial help, thanks to Horizon Tours, and to Meteb at Amazing Tours. In Al Ula, thanks to the two rawis (storytellers) at Dedan and to Mada'in Salih guide Hamad Alemam, as well as Bander. Also to Khalid in Najran.

In Kathmandu, thanks to Pawan, Roman and Rikesh of Himalayan Map House for their technical assistance. Thanks to Hugh Rhodes and Pete Gandy, who travelled with Bob in 1974.

And finally, thanks to the reader, who can help to keep this small guidebook updated for the benefit of future travellers.

Just filling in an 'empty quarter' page of the book: the 'well-dressed' authors at Dedan!

Contents

Highlights of Saudi Arabia

Traditional buildings in Al Balad, Old Jeddah

Visiting the markets in Al Balad

Al Ula Canyon

Mada'in Salih

Wadi Qaraqir canyon

Palace in Tayma

Shaqra old mud city

Ushaiger old city alley

Dumat al-Jandal: Marid Fort

Old Khaybar fort

White volcanoes – Al Bayda

Camels in the desert

Wabah Crater

Asir Mountains

Zee al-Ayn village

Abha: Amazing architecture in Al Basta district

Najran: Emarah Palace

Shafi Mosque in Al Balad, Jeddah

Deserts and Mountains

Outcrops en route from Madinah to Khaybar

High mountains and desert near Al Ula

Desert outcrops near Mada'in Salih

Sandstone outcrops near Mada'in Salih

Amazing jagged outcrops

Desert scenery between Khaybar and Al Ula

History & Culture

Jeddah: Modern city skyline

Dedan: ancient city outcrop

Remains of Dedan

Al Ula Tantora: historic mud city

Tomb at Mada'in Salih

Ancient diwan at Mada'in Salih

Tayma: historic Haddaj well

Ha'il: Qishlah Fort

Sakaka: Qasr Zaba'al

Rijal al-Ma: inside the museum

Abha: Abu Malha Palace

Najran: Al Aan Fort

Meeting the people

Inside the old souk in Jeddah

Relaxing in Al Balad, old Jeddah

Red Sea Palace Hotel: modern comforts next to the old city

A relaxing puff or two on a traditional hookah pipe

Mada'in Salih guide

Exploring Mada'in Salih

Winter at Tantora cafe, Al Ula

Admiring the view over Al Ula

Locals in Najran, Abu As Su'ud

Bir Hima wells, father & daughter

Friendly girls in Sakaka

Locals in Abha

Shopping for oranges

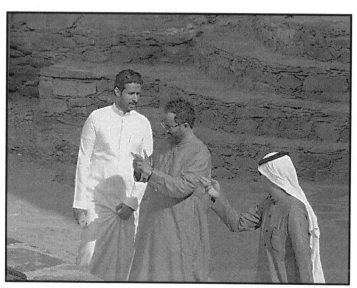

Selfies the world over!

On the road

Approaching Khaybar oasis

Steep descent ahead: low gear

Road down to Zee al-Ayn

'It ain't half hot mum' en route to Riyadh in 1974

Small towns, old vehicles, Shaqra in 1974

Modern cities, fast cars in 2019

Trekking options

Jebel Abiadh: the male white volcano

Jebel Qidr: the black volcano

Wabah Crater (trail descends on the left)

Trekking into Wadi Qaraqir

Hiking into the Jebel Hisma northern outcrops near Tabuk

Rugged mountains of the Asir

Picturesque villages in the Asir region

Preface

Although long on many adventure seeker's list of destinations, Saudi Arabia has remained off-limits to travellers for decades – until now. In late 2019 the Saudi authorities began issuing tourist visas for the first time. Previously only invited skilled expats, workers and pilgrims had been permitted entry. The vast country has a wealth of hidden and untapped treasures for discerning travellers – places like old Jeddah, Al Ula, Mada'in Salih, Wadi Qaraqir, Khaybar, Ushaiger, Ha'il, Al Jawf, Wabah (Al Waba) Crater, Zee al-Ayn, Rijal al-Ma, Najran and the Rub al-Khali desert or Empty Quarter, just for a start.

Amazingly, in 1974 Bob and two friends drove freely through the country in an old Land Rover as part of an overland trip from London to Kathmandu. A transit visa was possible then, obtained in Beirut before it blew apart with civil wars. Of course explorers and colonial emissaries did visit the 'secretive' country in the early 20th century. The exploits of Lawrence of Arabia and Wilfred Thesiger are well known in travellers' circles, but that is about all. The Saudi people today are quite familiar with the habits of foreigners, and a genuine hospitality is encountered.

Saudi Arabia is not the first country that comes to mind for a 'holiday', but early tourists are finding it to be a surprisingly charming and fascinating destination. Often misunderstood, it remains an enigma for most, and for that reason it is sure to be a much sought-after destination in the next few years.

Since the dawn of history, the country has been influenced mainly by its isolation and desert expanses. No major ancient civilisation really penetrated the deserts of the interior; only the coastal areas were known to outsiders and traders. It gave birth to one of the greatest religions of the world. Perhaps it is this profound history of isolation, etched into its fabric, that gives the country and its colourful people such a unique blend of ancient and modern, religion and culture. The population is diverse, a great melting pot of tribal peoples.

Today ancient traditions and ultra-modern development live side-by-side. The burgeoning cities are the equal of any in grandeur, modernisation and development. The desert is sublime – quiet, peaceful, dramatic, varied and beguiling. Where history reveals itself, the sights are astonishing: rock-carved tombs, ancient mud towns, striking mediaeval architecture, citadels and rock art that can be traced back aeons to the dawn of modern pastoralism.

There are many surprises in this once-lost horizon, with its sunny coastlines, ancient remains, deep gorges, towering outcrops and panoramic vistas, bustling streets and atmospheric souks.

The geography is astonishing, in the variety of the desert landscapes and the rugged topography of the mountains in the south. The exotic and romantic lure of the Empty Quarter is sure to entice many, where the endless expanse of rolling sand dunes has remained silent for centuries – a silence that few people in the modern era have experienced.

We spent only a few weeks in the country, but others will spend much longer, working or just exploring more, and enjoying the ambience of the country. Saudi Arabia, such an influential player in the world, is, it seems, now open for travellers (and maybe soon for desert trekkers).

This guide is really just an introductory window on the country. Saudi Arabia is such a vast land that it requires a lot of time and effort to see all the sights on offer. The road network is good and a small car adequate to travel thousands of kilometres across the country. Fuel costs next to nothing and car hire is cheap when arranged in advance. Having visited for just over two weeks at the end of 2019, we were drawn back again in February to explore more hidden corners of this extensive land, covering more than 11,000 kilometres in total over five weeks. This guide is a combination of our own two journeys and of the considerable amount of historical / geological / geographical information lodged on the internet.

Saudi Arabia will surely attract all those who have a sense of curiosity and are seeking to discover its many and varied charms.

Go soon!

Siân and Bob
Jeddah and Kathmandu 2020

Old Jeddah: Intriguing form of transport maybe?

Introduction

> Not all those who wander are lost.
> **Lord of the Rings, J R R Tolkien**

Apart from natural curiosity, visitors are starting to choose to come to Saudi Arabia for a variety of reasons. There is a certain appeal in being among the first visitors to explore a country. Having been so influential in the last century since the discovery of the black gold – oil – perhaps the country can see that a new future needs to be secured, and one way it seems is through tourism.

It is not an easy destination to visit yet; there are apartment-style hotels, but some are basic and hardly any of them are marked in English. In fact not many people speak English, other than some South Asian workers. Very few hotels have their own restaurants, and most do not even serve breakfast. Don't expect to find much traditional cuisine except in the more expensive hotels. Families do not commonly eat out together, so restaurants are rare; fast-food takeaways with separate entrances for men and women are the norm. Menus from local eateries are sometimes available for delivery to the hotel. Even then, vegetarians and vegans will find it hard-going. In a few places, the traditional hookah pipes can be seen.

Many new guests are keen to delve into the outstanding historic sites, a kaleidoscope of little-known civilisations reaching back thousands of years. Lovers of nature venture in search of the surprising diversity of the often-scarce flora and rare fauna that survive in the harsh desert environments. The mostly rare birds of Saudi are not easily spotted in the wild and neither are the desert creatures who forage a meagre living. The Arabian Oryx is again alive and well.

In the immediate future, trekkers might have to be patient to explore the lost canyons, fairytale turrets and outcrops that the deserts keep secret. But with most of the Sahara (Algeria – long a favourite, Libya, Niger and Mali) sadly off-limits, desert 'addicts' may well find a new dawn in Saudi Arabia.

It's quite a challenge for independent travellers to explore the country – the road network is exceedingly good, but the transport system is mainly dictated by the private motor car. Distances are vast and public transport relatively scarce. Those on organised tours will not suffer any privations, with good private transportation and vehicles to ferry them to the antiquities and sights beyond the cities. The vast nature of the country means that most visitors will experience only a brief glimpse of the country's secrets.

The capital Riyadh hardly reflects the real nature of the country, with its soaring skyscrapers and suburban sprawl. Jeddah gives visitors a more authentic feel for the country, with its bustling souks and streets in contrast with the sophisticated city scenes of the capital. The whispers around the ancient sites of long-gone civilisations inspire thought-provoking contemplation, while the cool breezes of the coastal dawn offer a different type of tranquillity. At day's end the fiery red sunsets over the shore and the intoxicating silence of the starry nights of the desert will not easily be forgotten.

****

Of course, any venture into little-tested new destinations presents some risks and dangers that unfamiliarity might pose – like the frenetic, sometimes undisciplined traffic! For most the cultural considerations must be paramount; it's so easy to offend without knowledge or forethought.

A trip to Saudi Arabia needs some preparation and informed planning by any prospective visitor. Part of this guide is devoted to those aspects; knowing certain things in advance makes travel a little easier. We too have travelled on a wing and a prayer in hope many times before and we too will not understand the country, its people, its culture and its traditions from only one recent visit.

The aim of this guide is not to detail every place, hotel, café or side trip, but to give an introduction to the country and what is on offer – something that for so many years has been unthinkable.

Approach to Wadi Qaraqir

BEFORE THE TRIP

Map of Saudi Arabia

List of maps

General background

Geography

The borders of Saudi Arabia extend roughly for around 2000km northwest to southeast from the Jordan and Iraq borders to Yemen and Oman. Its width ranges from 1200km – 1600km from the Red Sea to the Arabian Gulf. The country is divided into 13 provinces.

There are four generally distinct geographical regions: a narrow arid coastal plain along the Red Sea in the southwest, the western mountain chain, the vast central desert and the great sand seas of the Empty Quarter, mainly bordering Oman and northeast Yemen. The dominant feature of the country is the desert, which covers around 85% of the country.

Rising from the Red Sea, the mountain chain inland from the coast runs for about 1600km northwest to southeast from the Gulf of Aqaba to the Yemeni border. Its average width is roughly 50–100km west to east. The range rises from 1000m to an average height of nearly 3000m as it continues into Yemen.

Much of the upland zone inland is part of the Great Rift Valley that is tearing East Africa, including Djibouti, parts of Eritrea and Ethiopia, apart from the rest of the continent. It extends from Jordan down the Red Sea through Eritrea and Djibouti, continuing south into Kenya and Tanzania. This fault system gives rise to volcanic activity in all those countries, some still active, like the boiling cauldron of Erta Ale in Ethiopia and the dormant fissures and rifts of Kenya. However, the lava flows of the various areas further inland, called the harrats, are a separate volcanic rift system that threatens to break Saudi Arabia itself apart in aeons to come.

In the northwest the coastal range appears in a slightly lower and more fractured form, with sandstone base layers topped by ancient lava flows that form canyons and gullies. With weathering and erosion, the plateau has broken and shattered, often into square-shaped blocks with chequered-like corridors. Such features are present in the areas north of Madinah (Medina), inland from the Red Sea coast and particularly prominent around Al Ula. More volcanic features and ancient lava flows are interspersed with this plateau region, especially around and east of Khaybar. The mountains of the southwest Asir region receive more sustaining rains, making some of the region more fertile. The southern Red Sea coast is called the Tihama – a barren, hot and almost uninhabitable land.

The last major feature of the south and southeast is the vast Empty Quarter, with its extensive sand dunes and sand seas. South of the capital and extending for over 1500km east–west and 800km north–south, it's the largest area of purely sand in the world. It, of course, evokes romantic notions of how desolate a desert should be, with isolated oases of swaying palms and camel caravans. It's not quite like that now, but it has always had an inexplicable, magnetic pull for explorers.

Geology in brief

The main and surprising geological facts of interest are related to the recent (5–10 million years ago) volcanic activity that affected the country. These areas, known as harrats, experienced fast-moving lava flows. They are found across large areas of the northwest and western regions, northeast of Madinah, close to Tabuk and as far south as Makkah. There are more flows north of Taif and smaller areas a little further south adjacent to the southwest mountains.

The whole system is discontinuous at the surface but runs for around 600km north–south with variations east–west. Some, around Kishb, flowed as recently as 2 million years ago, while the most recent flows were near Madinah. This volcanic activity is not directly related to that of the Great Africa Rift system that runs from Jordan to Tanzania.

Lava flows in the Harrat Khaybar

Harrat Al-Uwayrid in the north is 10 million years old, while the fields around Khaybar are thought to be 5 million years old. Harrat Kishb is east of Khaybar and is the youngest. The basaltic lava has variations.

Climate

The climate for most of the country can generally be categorised as very hot and dry for most of the year. Temperatures are regularly above 40°C from March–November, with only a few months of cooler

47

conditions. In the depths of winter it may get down to freezing in the northern desert areas closer to Jordan and Iraq. Winds are common in the desert, with sandstorms that blanket the air at times.

The Gulf region is also exceedingly hot and humid for much of the year, with only the winter months giving any respite.

The southern mountains defy this rationale, with quite cold winters and snow on the highest summits and ridges. The Red Sea coast is humid, muggy and blisteringly hot for much of the year. Fog banks are a feature of the southern areas, with humid clouds rising up to almost 3000m. This feature also occurs on the Eritrean side of the Red Sea at times in the winter months.

The optimum time to visit Saudi Arabia is in the winter, from late November to late March. Temperatures in the desert during this time are bearable in the south and very pleasant further north.

Sample average daytime temperatures (°C)				
	Dec	March	June	September
Riyadh	20	26	41	40
Jeddah	23	25	33	31
Makkah	24	27	35	34
Dammam	16	21	34	32
Tabuk	18	25	38	37
Abha	19	23	31	29

Natural history

With so few visitors to the country, there is not a lot of information about its natural history. Some environmental projects are beginning to take shape. Along with tourism, conservation is likely to develop to protect wildlife and areas of natural beauty, with a view to creating more national parks and conservation areas.

Plants

With not so many climatic zones, Saudi Arabia has limited and less varied plant life than regions with more seasons. That said, there are over 3500 species of plant recorded, with over 1000 types just in the wetter Asir region. This area, where fog persists due to the humid clouds rising up the escarpments, has cloud rainforest zones.

Botanists will find quite a variety of plants even in the desert. The arid coastal areas have few surviving natural areas, but occasional flash floods flow from the mountains down the dry river gorges to the sea, allowing some of nature's wonders to bloom temporarily.

A few hardy trees survive in the White Volcanoes area

Palm trees grow in profusion where underground and surface water exist, producing delicious dates.

Agriculture dominates the lower slopes of the mountains, although the need for housing is cutting into the available good fertile areas. reducing the supply of good land for growing. Dry, low bush and Mediterranean scrub characterise the rural areas between towns and villages. Acacias are found along the Tihama slopes with tamarisks and palm trees in the desert wadis. Some of the higher hills of the Asir mountains have stony, terraced fields, where trees offer sanctuary to birdlife and a few wild animals. The upper areas of the mountains are mostly bare, with dry stony slopes and little vegetation other than hardy, tough grasses.

The Rub al-Khali desert has a mere 37 recorded species of plants.

Animals

Saudi Arabia is home to an incredibly adaptable population of rare mammals and birds. The fauna is limited to those species that can survive the harsh desert climate. Such creatures like the tahr, Arabian wolf found in the Tabuk region. Fennec, red fox, caracal, striped hyena, rock hyrax and cape hare are some creatures that are found but rarely seen. The sand cat has adapted to live in the scorching deserts. The Arabian leopard is an endangered species found in the Asir mountains. Hamadrayas baboons are found in huge numbers along the roads of the Asir hills.

Hamadrayas baboon group

The Arabian oryx has been hunted almost to extinction but re-introduction programs are underway in the Mahazat as-Sayd reserve. Lion, cheetah and Syrian wild ass once roamed the region before becoming extinct in most of the Middle East. Domestic animals – mainly camels, horses, sheep, goats, mules and even a few donkeys – are found in varying numbers across the country. Saudi Arabia imports camels from Sudan across the Red Sea.

Camels coming up for a feed at Harrat Khaybar

Birds

Although a vast area in size, the country's climate limits the variety and number of birds. Sandgrouse, quails, eagles, buzzards and larks can be found. Gulls and pelicans frequent the Red Sea coast.

The Red Sea is also a flyway for thousands of migratory birds between Africa and Europe, including flamingos, pelicans and cormorants. In addition, the once-hunted bird populations include elegant herons, storks and cranes, various species of pigeons and doves. Birds of prey – eagles, hawks, vultures, falcons and buzzards – are rarely seen. Across the skies of the Asir mountains there is a chance to see vultures, eagles and barbary falcons. Yemen linnet, thrush and warbler live here, as well as the rarer African paradise flycatcher. The very rare hamerkop is only found in the Wadi Turabah Nature reserve in the Makkah region southeast of Taif.

General history of Arabia and the Middle East

The history of Saudi Arabia is to some extent linked to that of the Middle East. The great civilisations of the Middle East did not generally penetrate significantly into the inhospitable lands south of Jordan and Iraq. The trade in frankincense probably had the greatest influence on the Arabian Peninsula. It is generally agreed that human development began in Africa, but the development of the earliest civilisations took place across the Middle East. The Eastern Mediterranean has a recorded human history stretching back over 8,000 years, but few of the great civilisations actually turned their attentions to the desert wastes to the south.

Long before the civilisations of the Middle East, the region of Saudi Arabia probably had a much wetter climate. This changed to a more arid weather pattern around 6000 years ago. Over the next 5000 years the climate dried and desert took hold. Evidence suggests that the inhabitants practised basic pastoralism and later adopted a more nomadic lifestyle.

The first people came from Iraq, where the Babylonian and Sumerian civilisations spread across the Middle East. Evidence exists of settlements along the Mediterranean shore, notably at Byblos in Lebanon. Around 3000BC a wave of people moved into the region. They would become known as the Phoenicians. The Phoenicians were followed by the Amorites and Arameans. The Hyksos period (18th century BC) is a more obscure period of history.

Between 1550BC and 1300BC, the Egyptian civilisation expanded from the River Nile as a major power of the region. Around 1300BC, the Hittite Empire also expanded south from central Turkey into the Levant, although mainly into the area of modern-day Syria. The Phoenician trading civilisation along the coast was at its zenith in Lebanon from 1200BC for three centuries. Confined to the coast, the Phoenicians' main centres were Byblos, Tyre, Sidon and Berytus (Beirut). During this period the Philistines migrated to Lebanon, probably from the Aegean. They overthrew the Hittites and were the ancestors of the Palestinian people.

The Assyrian Empire arrived from the region of Persia around 1000BC. They in turn were defeated by the Babylonians under King Nebuchadnezzar. The next wave of intruders who rode in from Persia were the Achaemenids, around 540BC. Little remains of these waves of marauders in the region today.

Alexander the Great swept across much of Asia from the Mediterranean to India around 332BC. The following Seleucid rulers were finally defeated by the Romans in 64BC. Only Rome would have an impact of any consequence on Arabia.

However, one civilisation did have a significant influence on northwest Saudi Arabia. The Nabatean civilisation, centred on southern Jordan and almost as far south as Medina, lasted in Saudi Arabia from the 1st century BC to the end of the 1st century AD, when Rome engulfed its empire.

The Nabateans

The Nabateans were probably one of several tribes who lived a nomadic existence in the Arabian region. Scholars think that they moved into the northwest area of Arabia and into Jordan between 6th and 4th centuries BC. As they consolidated their lands, so the trade flourished, and the kingdom became rich. Their domains extended eventually from Jordan to the Hejaz and even as far north as Damascus, which they controlled from 85–71BC.

Perhaps the best reference to the Nabateans comes from the Greek historian Diodorus Siculus around 30BC. He found information from one of Alexander the Great's generals, Hieronymus, recorded about 300 years earlier. In this reference the chronicler describes the Nabateans (of Petra) as the people who lived in the desert wastes and dug cisterns and wells that they hid from sight. This ensured that any intruders perished for lack of water. Diodorus also suggests that the Assyrians, the Medes or the Persians managed to conquer the early Nabateans.

After the death of Alexander, Antigonus took the Levant and sought to extend his domains to the Nabatean areas. They had already grown wealthy from the trade of frankincense and myrrh from Yemen to the port on the Gaza coast, from where it could be shipped to Europe. Antigonus attacked the Nabatean enclave of Petra in 312BC, but was very soon repulsed by the Nabateans.

The Greeks continued to attack Petra and sought the wealth of bitumen around the Dead Sea, which they used for embalming. This time the forces of Hieronymus were repulsed by the 'Arabs', who were most probably the Nabateans. Conflicts between the Ptolemites and the Seleucids to the north enabled the Nabateans to expand their kingdom elsewhere. From the middle of the 3rd century BC the Nabateans consolidated their growing empire. A recent discovery, called the Milan Papyrus, suggests that the Nabateans already had wealth and power in the region of Jordan. The first reference to any Nabatean king was of Aretas I, who is mentioned in chronicles in 168–169 and in inscriptions recovered in the Negev desert.

In the 2nd century the Nabateans introduced coinage to facilitate trade. Meanwhile, another Nabatean king, Obodas, defeated local tribes, including the Judeans, in 93BC at the battle of Gadara, but this merely made them vulnerable to the mighty Seleucids to the north. Obodas, however, did defeat the Seleucids and the Greeks. King Obodas was finally laid to rest at Aydat, a temple built for the king in the Negev.

The constant threat from the north forced the Nabateans to seek out new centres, and thus they established the settlement of Hegra (Mada'in Salih) in Arabia, far to the south of Petra. From 87BC–62BC King Aretas III expanded the territory further but aroused the concerns of Rome. The Nabatean civilisation depended on trade; as well as frankincense from Yemen, they also exchanged goods such as gold, iron, copper, ivory, fabrics and even medicinal products. Trade flowed as far as China, India and southern Europe. The more the Nabateans prospered, the more apprehensive Rome became.

When Julius Caesar was assassinated in 44BC, the Parthians and Persian gained the upper hand and the Nabateans sided with the Parthians. The Parthians, however, were soon defeated by Rome and Petra had to pay tribute to Rome. King Aretas IV (9AD–40AD) manage to prosper by enhancing the settlements along the Frankincense route of the Hejaz to Yemen, thus maintaining the Nabatean wealth. Eventually around 70AD the Nabateans, fearful of Rome, sought to ally themselves with the Romans.

It was only a matter of time now before Rome took over the lands of the Nabateans. In 106AD, during the reign of the Roman emperor Trajan, the last recognised king of the Nabatean kingdom, Rabbel II Soter, died. The Romans claimed Petra, calling it Arabia Petrea. As trade patterns changed with routes via Palmyra (in Syria), and as ships began to sail to the southern ports of Arabia, Petra declined. By the end of the 1st century AD Mada'in Salih was already in decline. In the 4th century AD the Nabateans left Petra and with it their civilisation ceased.

The Nabatean capital in Jordan: Petra

The Sassanid Persian Empire reached west into Syria thereafter, but not into Arabia. It was during this time that the warrior queen Zenobia expanded an empire that took control of much of Syria, along with some of Egypt and Palestine, with its capital at Palmyra. Hers was a short-lived reign. Queen Zenobia was defeated by Aurelian and eventually ended up in Rome, where she met an unknown fate.

The next significant event, although of little consequence at the time, was the coming of Christianity, as it spread out from the Holy Land. Initially Christianity had little impact, but much later it was to dominate the region's history. The Byzantine Emperor Constantine converted to Christianity in 313AD, marking a new period across the whole of the western Middle East. Constantinople (Istanbul) became a great rival to Rome in Christendom.

For the next 400 years, power fluctuated between Byzantium and the Persian invaders. However, it was not the Persians who would eventually have the greatest impact on the region, but a new religion sweeping up from the deserts of Arabia.

The new religion that rose up in the 7th century was Islam. The Prophet Muhammad (peace be upon him – pbuh) was born in Makkah around 570AD; he received revelations from God in 610. He moved north to Madinah in 622, where he continued to espouse his teachings that were to unite the tribes of the Arabian lands. He died in 632AD and was laid to rest in Madinah.

The cities of Makkah (Mecca) and Madinah (Medina) became the most important religious sites for Muslims, with the Masjid al-Haram (Grand Mosque) and the black stone of the Kaaba the focal points for pilgrims. In Madinah, the Masjid al-Nabawi (the Prophet's Mosque) marks the location of the tomb of the Prophet.

After a period of confusion and brief conflict, known as the 'wars of apostasy' or 'ridda' wars, the first caliph was appointed. The first Caliph was Abu Bakr Abdullah ibn-Uthman; he was one of the first to convert to Islam. Being rich from business, he gave his wealth to the cause of Muhammad. He travelled with Muhammad to Madinah in 622 and was active during the conflicts of Badr and Uhud.

Abu Bakr assumed the cause of expanding the domains of the new religion. He extended the faith across Arabia, despite resistance by the Sassanids and by Byzantium. His efforts led to the Muslim conquest of Persia and the Levant. He served as Caliph for just two years and only lived until 634.

Umar (Omar) ibn al-Khattab became the second Caliph in 634; he was a pious and devoted man. Together with three generals, he rapidly expanded the lands of Islam. They vanquished the Sassanids in the years 642–644 and conquered Persia, but Umar was eventually killed in battle by a Persian.

Uthman ibn al Affan was the third Caliph; he was assassinated in 656. Uthman (Osman) was a son-in-law of the Prophet. He is credited with being the one who ordered the compilation of the Quran (Koran). The lands of Islam expanded further under Uthman, to include Persia by 650 and Khorasan (Afghanistan) in 651. His reign was not without conflict, and widespread disagreement with his stewardship eventually led to his assassination. The First Fitna revolts, 656–661, followed the assassination of Uthman. The great schism in Islam began under his reign, when followers of Ali believed that Uthman had strayed from the right path, although Ali himself was not a party to this.

Ali ibn Abi Talib became the fourth Caliph; his tenure lasted from 656–661. He was a cousin and son-in-law of the Prophet Muhammad. He was born in the sanctuary of the Kaaba in Makkah. He also migrated to Madinah, where he married Muhammad's daughter Fatima. He was assassinated in Kufra by a Kharijite. These Caliphs were collectively called the 'al-khuafa ar Rashidun' or the 'rightly guided' ones.

Already a rift was developing between the those who followed the Caliphs, and those who believed that power should rest with the direct descendants of the Prophet, like Ali. Later Ali's son, Hussain, continued the disputes between the two warring groups, and he too was killed as he and his family battled a large army of the Caliph. Hussain's body was left where he fell at Karbala (680AD), in modern Iraq, which is now a holy site for the Shia.

This disagreement was never to heal, and it split the Muslim world as it still does today. The Shiites are led by their imams, who have a spiritual significance, unlike the clerics of the Sunni branch. Ali became the first imam and Hussain the third. Later the Shia adopted Ali as the true descendant of Muhammad.

Concurrently the descendants of the Caliphs, the Omayyads, consolidated the religion with a capital at Damascus. After 661 the Omayyad empire took root and spread the word of Islam across the Middle East and North Africa.

Muawiyah I became the first of the Omayyad rulers to develop Makkah, adding houses and wells. Makkah began to attract poets, artisans and musicians, but never outshone Madinah in these years where the aristocracy were prominent.

Arab advances resulted in vast territories being converted to Islam, from the Middle East to North Africa, and from Spain into southern France. Damascus fell in 635, followed by Jerusalem in 636. Syria and Palestine were overrun in 637, along with Mesopotamia in the same year. Egypt succumbed in 641, Libya in 647, Tunisia in 667 and Algeria by 680AD. The Arabs mixed with the indigenous Berbers of the Maghreb in North Africa. Two years later the lands of Morocco became followers of Islam.

To the east the migration was equally fast, reaching the gates of India by 694. Central Asia was won between 704 and 724AD. Although various successes were achieved across Turkey, it was not until 717 that victory ensued. The religion spread east from India and beyond to Indonesia. It could not last, and in 732AD the Arabs lost their lands in France with the battle of Tours and defeat by Charles Martel.

The next major incident was under Yazid I, when the revolt of Abd Allah bin al Zubair forced intervention from Syria. The Kaaba was damaged in the revolt and then in 747AD a Yemeni-led incursion seized Makkah. This was put down by Muawiyah II. The Omayyad (Umayyad) Empire declined by 750AD, leaving the Arab tribes to themselves.

Omayyad Mosque, Damascus 2010

Meanwhile, in the Middle East the Abbasids took power, moving the capital of the new regime from Damascus to Kufa in 751AD.

The Caliphate under Al Mansour moved the capital from Kufa to Baghdad around 160km north in 762AD. The Abbasids expanded the routes to Makkah and Madinah, developing resources to sustain pilgrims along the way, later called the Darb Zubaydah.

A major oasis en route was that of Fayd, where a stone-built castle remains. The Abbasid Empire lasted until 980AD, when the Fatimids from Egypt took power.

Fayd castle ruins

Stunning oasis wells like that of Sisra in Sakaka

Twelvers
The twelfth Imam (known as the Hidden Imam) had a big impact on the Shia in the 10th century. It is said that God took the Imam into hiding and that he will reappear at the end of time. He is also known as the Mahdi. Many Shia believe in the Hidden Imam and they are known as the 'Twelver Shiites'. Most immediately think of the Mahdi as the one who fought General Gordon in Khartoum, but that is another story.

From the 10th century the Hashemite Sharifs controlled the cities of Makkah and Madinah, later extending their domains to include most of the Hejaz region in the 13th century. At the same time, various empires of the Middle East had some control over the lands. These were the Abbasids of Baghdad and the Fatimids, Ayyubids and Mamluks of Egypt.

In the Middle Ages, hostilities between the Muslims and the interloping crusaders masked the Muslim split. Before 1500 Persia was a Sunni-following region, but soon after this the Safavid Turkic dynasty of the Mongol lineage converted it to Shia. Persia was sandwiched between the Sunni Ottomans and the Mughals of India, who were also Sunni.

Holding control of all the historic sights of Christianity, the Muslims next faced an onslaught from Europe. It began with a call to arms from Pope Urban II in 1095. He called for the restoration of Christianity in its birthplace of Bethlehem and the capturing of the Church of the Holy Sepulchre in Jerusalem. The Crusaders were a generally violent mass of invaders and finally took Jerusalem in 1099. The crusaders built the famous castles of Krak des Chevaliers in Syria near the northeastern border of Lebanon, and Kerak in Jordan, as well as the smaller sites in Lebanon at Byblos and Sidon.

The greatest foe of the Crusaders was Saladin (1138–1193), who recaptured much of the ground they had taken. The epic battles between Saladin and Richard the Lionheart are legendary and concluded with a peace treaty signed in 1192. The Crusaders kept the coast, including Lebanon, while the Muslims retained the tracts across the mountains in Syria and Jordan. The Ayyubids and the Turkish Mamluks took over the lands of the Muslims.

The Mamluks ruled from their capital in Cairo after 1250 and had evicted the Crusaders from most of the coastal lands by 1302. It was the Mongols who next intervened briefly, when Tamerlane reached Aleppo and Damascus, finally ending the rule of the Mamluk Turks. The Mongols had little interest in the region soon departed when the Ottoman Turks took power in the early 16th century.

The Ottoman era began in Arabia when Selim I took Makkah and Madinah in 1517. Their domains included the Hejaz region, the Asir mountains and the Al Ahsa (Al Hasa) region on the Gulf coast. They never attempted to control all of the Arabian Peninsula and did not even assert their power over the holy cities, leaving them, like other empires, to the Sharifs of the cities. They did retain a garrison in Makkah. In the 17th century the Ottomans lost control in the eastern Al Ahsa region, though they still held most of the Levant and south into Saudi Arabia, as well as in the Balkans.

In 1744 the first Saudi dynasty arose when Muhammad ibn Saud from Ad Dir'iyah (Diriyah) near modern Riyadh joined forces with Muhammad ibn Abd-al-Wahhab to expand the Wahabi movement. It still influences the country greatly. The Saud rulers were in conflict to varying degrees with the empires of Egypt and the Ottomans. Between 1786 and 1816 the Saudis did not always hold total power and in 1818 the Ottomans took control. The Turkish Sultan Mustafa IV requested Mohammad Ali Pasha to reclaim the area of Saudi Arabia, sending his sons Tusum Pasha and Ibrahim Pasha to do this. The Al Saud dynasty moved in 1824 to gain control over parts of the country, that was mainly the Najd region. This was the beginning of the second Saudi State.

The Saudis did not retain control long before coming into conflict with the Rashidis of Ha'il. In fact the power struggle lasted years, until 1891, the end of the second Arabian dynasty. The Al Saud were pushed into exile in the region of Kuwait by the Al Rashid. The Egyptians controlled the Hejaz until 1840, but departed as the Ottomans arrived. The Sharifs still maintained control over Makkah and Madinah though at the same time. Although the Ottomans retained overall control, in reality they held little outright power. That continued to be held by tribal rulers, which included the Al Saud who had returned from exile in 1902.

In 1902 Abdul Aziz Al Saud left Kuwait to continue the conflict with the Al Rashids and captured Riyadh. In his quest, Al Saud utilised the forces of the Ikhwan or Wahhabi Bedouin tribes. Sultan Bjad Al Otaibi and Faisal al Duwaish led the forces. In 1906 Abdul Aziz removed the Rashid from the Najd, forcing the Turks to recognise this fact. Abdul Aziz then moved on the eastern regions of Al Ahsa in 1913. Having avoided the disputes of the Arab revolt in the west with the Ottomans, he pursued his struggle with the Al Rashid of the north.

World War I broke out in 1914 and changed the course of events even in Arabia. After 400 years, the Ottoman empire finally crumbled; the Turks sided with Germany and the Arabs with the British. By 1915 Britain recognised the need for a Pan-Arab renaissance. The Arabs were represented by Sharif Hussein bin Ali, a Hashemite.

Britain agreed to recognise the Arab aspirations in exchange for help against the Ottomans in Saudi Arabia. The aim was to secure an Arab domain from Syria to Yemen.

This revolt began with the Bedouin tribes, although the Al Saud were not part of it, still being consumed by disputes with the Al Rashid. When the Ottomans were defeated after WWI, in 1918 the colonial powers Britain and France failed to live up to their promises of a pan-Arab state. Hussein was left with the Hejaz but later the British backed the Al Saud. It was then that Lawrence of Arabia effectively, if inadvertently, encouraged the Arabs to revolt to claim their independence.

Thomas Edward Lawrence (T. E.)

Lawrence was born in 1888 in Tremadog, in Wales. Born out of wedlock, his guardians adopted the name of Lawrence. The family moved to Scotland and then to Brittany in France. Lawrence went to school in Oxford, later reading history at Jesus College from 1907–1910. He then went to the Middle East as an archaeologist. After his time in Saudi Arabia detailed in the history section, he retreated from public life. During the next few years he wrote the book, Seven Pillars of Wisdom, detailing his time with the Arabs in Saudi Arabia. His activities in the Hejaz were given greater credence by American journalist, Lowell Thomas, helping the story to become more familiar. Lawrence sided with Sharif Hussein, who had occupied Makkah against the Ottomans. Madinah endured a long siege by Hussein, which did not end until after the armistice of January 1919. In all, the siege lasted two years and seven months. Lawrence also spent periods as an enlisted man in the Royal Air Force. He died in 1935 in a motorcycle accident in Dorset, a controversial figure to the end.

Between 1910 and 1914 Lawrence had worked as an archaeologist at the British museum of Carchemish in Syria during the Ottoman period. When WWI broke out, he volunteered for the army and was posted to Egypt under General Allenby. In 1916 he was sent to Saudi Arabia and became embroiled with the Arab Revolt in the western region of the Hejaz. He collaborated with Emir Faisal, a local leader, and became a liaison officer with the Arab forces against the Turks. This led to his military actions with Faisal against the Ottomans. The Arabs captured Damascus in autumn 1918. Subsequently the nationalists were snubbed, as the colonial powers France and Britain carved up the Middle East.

Allenby promoted him to major and then to colonel. After the end of the war he joined the Foreign Office, working with Faisal. The failure of the British to keep their promises to the Bedouins led to bitter acrimony when the colonials backed the Al Saud.

Lawrence was offered the Victoria Cross and a knighthood but refused both in sympathy with his friends in the Hejaz.

In Arabia, after WWI the Ikhwan movement next turned their attention to the south, capturing the Asir regions in 1920. In 1921 the Al Saud finally defeated the Al Rashid in the north. Meanwhile Hussein bin Ali was left alone in the Hejaz; that is until the British withdrew in 1923. A meeting was called in Riyadh in 1924 to discuss the boycott of the pilgrimage routes from Najd in contravention of the Shari'a. The Ikhwan moved on Makkah to root out the practices that it deemed to be anti-Islam. By the beginning of 1926 the Ikhwan had taken the Hejaz, with Abdul Aziz pronouncing himself 'king' of the region as well as the Hajd.

King Faisal

Faisal was born to King Abdul Aziz Al Saud in 1906. His mother was Tarfa bint Abdullah bin Abdullatif Al Sheikh, whom Abdul Aziz had married in 1902 after capturing Riyadh. With a good command of English at the age of only 13, he was sent to Britain to attempt to negotiate with Lord Curzon to promote Abdul Aziz as the rightful leader of the country. After three fruitless months and a lot of manoeuvring to meet influential people, such as Princess Mary, Harry St John Philby who backed the Al Saud leadership, Winston Churchill and others, the astute young prince managed to meet Curzon, and through his persuasive powers, the British decided to back Abdul Aziz. The story is very well told in the recently released film **Born a King**, made by a joint Saudi-Anglo-Spanish production. Faisal became king in 1964 and steered the country through the oil crisis. He was assassinated in 1973 by a nephew.

In 1927 the British recognised the independence of the domains held by Abdul Aziz in the Treaty of Jeddah. The Wahabis wanted to expand their powers into Jordan, Iraq and Kuwait, but Abdul Aziz was averse to any further conflict with the colonials. In 1929 during the Battle of Sabilla, the Ikhwan movement was defeated. The borders with Jordan, Iraq and Kuwait were defined and in 1930 the Kingdom of Saudi Arabia was finally established. In 1934, disputes with Yemen were ended, and in the Treaty of Taif the borders were mostly defined.

In 1938 oil was discovered in vast quantities in the country's eastern region and exploitation began in 1941. Oil began to flow by 1949. In 1945 King Abdul Aziz concluded an agreement with Franklin D Roosevelt to guarantee the state of Saudi Arabia in exchange for a flow of oil to America. This meeting took place on the USS Quincy in the Suez Canal. King Abdul Aziz died in 1953, to be succeeded by King Saud, his son.

Harry St John Bridger Philby

An extraordinary adventurer, St John Philby was born in Ceylon in 1885 and later studied Oriental Languages at Cambridge. He was posted to Lahore in 1908. In 1915 he was recruited into service in Baghdad in the financial branch. In reality he was involved with the Arab revolts against the Turks and in protecting the vital waterways near Basra. In 1917 he went to Arabia to be the head of mission attached to Abdul Aziz Al Saud. Gradually Philby came to favour the Al Sauds over the Hashemite Hussain bin Ali, the Sharif of Mecca, whom the British favoured. Philby was instrumental in preventing conflict between the Al Saud and the Sharif of Mecca and, through the diplomacy of the young Prince Faisal, the Al Saud were entrusted as guardians of the country. He converted to Islam in 1930 and soon after journeyed along the Yemen border and into the Rub al-Khali, where he later discovered the Wabar impact craters in 1932 while in search of the Ubar oasis. His book The Empty Quarter was published in 1933. He lived much of his life in Arabia and died in Beirut in 1960, where his son, the double agent Kim Philby, was staying.

In 1962 a war broke out between the royalists and the republicans in neighbouring Yemen. In the event the Egyptians backed the republicans and the Saudis the royalists. In 1964 King Faisal took power from his incumbent half-brother. After the six-day war in 1967, Egypt withdrew its troops from Yemen. Saudi Arabia continued its economic aid to Jordan, Egypt and Syria. Saudi Arabia was instrumental in the formation of the oil cartel OPEC and moderated oil prices in the 1970s. Following the 1973 war, oil prices rose dramatically, making the kingdom prosperous and more influential.

In 1975 King Faisal was assassinated by his nephew and was succeeded by King Khalid. The wealth of the nation continued to grow. King Khalid died in 1982, to be followed by King Fahd, who established ever stronger ties with America. He died suddenly in 1995 and Crown Prince Abdullah took control. The various conflicts of the Middle East involving Iraq have influenced recent history, as is well known. In 2015 King Abdullah died and was succeeded by King Salman, who continues to be the head of state of the country.

Painting of Abdul Aziz Al Saud in Masmak Fort

People of Saudi Arabia

Today it is almost impossible to define who the 'real' Saudi Arabian people are, since they are collectively the tribes of Arabia today under the Saudi Royal family. Saudi men wear the traditional long white robe (*thawb* or *thobe*), with a red and white scarf (*keffiyeh*) held on with a black rope (*agal*) around the head. The women wear a black floor-length gown (*abaya*) and often the head-covering (*niqab*), with only a slit revealing the eyes. Surprisingly, few children are seen on the streets. The dress code for women has recently been relaxed, but most women continue to wear the same clothing.

A sizeable immigrant population has added a new dynamism to the economy and the country. Most are Muslims from across the Islamic world; the majority are Pakistanis, Bangladeshis, Yemenis and Afghans, plus Indian Muslims and Kashmiris. Egyptians, Sudanese and Somalis are the main migrants from Africa.

Friendly truckers are everywhere

Cultural aspects

Saudi Arabia has such a rich cultural heritage that you will probably only be able to scratch the surface. An understanding of local culture and history will go a long way towards enriching your experience.

Before you leave home, find out as much information as you can about the region. The more you know and respect the places you plan to visit, the less likely you are to disrupt local culture when you get there, and the more you will get out of your trip. Travelling carries responsibilities as well as bringing pleasure – dress in a manner to suit the different cultures; respect people's dignity and wishes, particularly when taking photographs; respect religious sites and artefacts. Do your bit for the environment, which only now is being addressed across the region.

It is impossible to learn the spoken word of all these differing groups, but any usage of even the most basic words will open doors and enable greater interaction. Despite the cultural divide, most people are welcoming, interested and lively.

One of the subjects most guaranteed to cause inadvertent offence or misunderstanding is that of religion. Learning about Islam and its etiquette will certainly improve any exchanges. That said, the people whom we met in the country could not have been more welcoming.

The nature of Islam in Saudi Arabia is generally more conservative than in some Arab regions. This means that visitors should respect local traditions and culture. Clothing, together with general appearance, is the one thing that defines your approach and can have negative as well as positive impacts.

Traditional buildings in Al Balad, Old Jeddah

Religion

The latest official figures suggest that 75–85% of Saudi Arabian citizens are Sunni Muslims, while 10–15% are Shia. More than 30% of the population are foreign workers, and most of them are also Muslims.

Islam

Virtually all the population follows Islam, Saudi Arabia being its place of origin. Most of the country is Sunni, but there are a few Shia communities, mainly in the east and in the far southwest. Islam has followers across most of the Middle East, in Syria, Jordan, Lebanon, Palestine, Iraq, Turkey and Egypt.

As well as the countries along the north African coast that adhere to Islam, a surprising number of sub-Saharan countries also have substantial numbers, if not all of their population, observing the religion. Islam spread south across the Sahara with the caravan routes from Egypt, Libya, Tunisia, Algeria, and Morocco after its founding in the middle of the 7th century in Saudi Arabia.

There are five main pillars of Islam. These are:

Witness (**shahadah**): submission to God (Allah) and acceptance that Muhammad is his prophet.

Prayer (**salat**): five times a day, at sunrise, midday, afternoon, sunset and evening. Before praying, Muslims must wash head, hands and feet. They can pray in any place that is clean and not polluted, and they must face Makkah (Mecca). On Fridays at midday, it is more beneficial to pray collectively at a mosque. Otherwise they may pray alone, wherever they may be. Men and women pray separately.

Alms giving (**zakat**): according to the Quran (Koran), faith in God should be expressed by doing good to others. Once a year, a devout Muslim should give 2.5% of his money to others in need.

Pilgrimage (**hajj**): At least once during his lifetime, it is a sacred duty for every Muslim to go to the Ka'aba, the sacred mosque in Makkah (Mecca). This should be done ideally between the seventh and tenth days of the month of Zuul-Hijja, the twelfth month of the Muslim year. This is usually between March and July, depending on the moon. The hajj includes, among other things, the *tawaf*, seven anticlockwise circuits of the Ka'aba, prostrations at the site of Abraham, and the sacrifice of either a sheep or a camel, depending on one's wealth. This meat is given to the poor. The pilgrimage ends with another feast, the Eid al-Adha, after which the pilgrim must visit the tomb of the prophet in the holy city of Madinah (Medina).

Fasting (**sawm**): the month of Ramadan is a holy month, when all Muslims must fast from dawn till dusk. If they are ill or travelling, or if they are pregnant women, they are permitted to postpone the fast until they are well. Elderly people and young children are excused from the fast. The purpose of the fast is to teach discipline to the soul. Eid al-Fitr is when the fast ends and all Muslims celebrate with a great feast – sheep and goats are not lucky, as hundreds of them are ritually slaughtered on this special day.

The Prophet Muhammad (Peace be upon him)

The Prophet Muhammad was born in 570AD into a Hashemite faction of the Quraysh tribe. He was born into a poor family of the Quraysh tribe. His father died before he was born, and he was raised by his grandfather and later by his uncle. Muhammad worked with the camel caravans that traded with Syria, the Mediterranean and as far away as the Indian Ocean coast. Muhammad gained a reputation for his honesty and sincerity and began working for a merchant woman, Khadija. Muhammad and Khadija were married and gave birth to several children. Being already a pious man Muhammad visited the sacred sites in Makkah. According to Islamic folklore it was in a cave on Jebel al Nour in 610 that Muhammad began receiving divine revelations from God through Archangel Jibra'il (Gabriel). Some of the revelations occurred in a cave on Mount Hira that led him becoming the Prophet Muhammad.

According to Islamic tradition his wife Khadija was the first person to believe, along with friend Abu Bakr, who would become the first Caliph and the one accepted by the Sunni as the rightful heir. Muhammad soon had a following and as his message spread so the tribal leaders in Makkah feared his teachings, which included the condemning of idol worship and paganism. His own tribe the Quraysh, guardians of the Kaaba, especially feared this new movement. After 13 years in 622 the Prophet and his followers moved to Madinah as threats grew against them. The conflict continued until the battle of Uhud when neither side triumphed. It was not until 627 in the Battle of the Trench (ditch) that the forces of Muhammad became more powerful. In 628 the followers of Muhammad returned to Makkah but were blocked by the Quraysh. The treaty of Hudaybiyyah allowed a tense peace but was violated by the Quraysh after 2 years. The superior forces of Muhammad marched on Makkah and peace ensured.

Following the conflicts with Makkah, the Prophet made his own pilgrimage to the city and delivered his last sermon at Mount Arafat. He died in June 632 and was buried in al-Masjid an-Nabawi, now the Mosque of the Prophet in Madinah, built by Muhammad.

Some more basic tenets of Islam are: the Quran (Koran) is the word of God; Muhammad (pbuh) is his prophet; the Sunna is the right way of life, which represents everything that the prophet Muhammad did or said. The books of Hadith record the Sunna, the way to live. Note that the Sunna is the guidance given by Muhammad; it is not the same as the Quran, which is the direct word of God. The Quran and the Sunna together are known as the al-Asl, the foundation of Islam. A madrasa is an Islamic school.

Muhammad's daughter was Fatima. Ali was his cousin. Muhammad favoured Ali as his successor, and married Fatima to Ali. Those who follow Ali are known as Shia Muslims.

Other religions in Saudi Arabia are rare, but a few migrant workers may follow other faiths.

Festivals

Most festivals in Saudi Arabia relate to religious celebrations. Muslims observe Ramadan and Eid al-Fitr at the end of the month-long fast. Those who get to the Hajj celebrate Eid al-Adha at its conclusion.

Basic customs

In general, the people are extremely friendly and welcoming to a stranger; sometimes almost to an embarrassing degree. However, visitors should observe a few basic customs.

Non-Muslims are not allowed into any mosques. Non-believers might be invited into homes across the country, but shoes are certainly not permitted inside. Women should not offer to shake hands with any man unless he offers his hand first. Foreigners, men and women, should wear conservative dress. Female visitors should wear a long-sleeved gown or tunic and carry a headscarf or shawl, which might best be worn most of the time.

Helping the people

Although the gulf between rich and poor is quite wide in Saudi Arabia, there is not the abject poverty seen in other parts of the Middle East or the Indian subcontinent. There is definitely no air of malaise. The familiar big donor organisations and charities are absent as the country has its own systems for charity.

Sustainable tourism

Tourism in Saudi Arabia is in its infancy, meaning some tolerance might need to be employed as the new programmes are implemented. The conservation of the architectural and historic heritage is already being developed. Preservation of nature in the mountain regions is in the spotlight, as tourism development is the latest policy objective.

PRACTICALITIES

Time and calendar

> The timeless in you is aware of life's timelessness. And knows that yesterday is but today's memory and tomorrow is today's dream.
> ***The Prophet*, Gibran Khalil Gibran**
> (Lebanese poet philosopher)

Saudi Arabia is 3hrs ahead of GMT.

Getting to Saudi Arabia

www.saudiarabiavisa.com

By air
The following airlines serve Saudi Arabia from Europe, Asia and Africa:
Air Algerie via Algiers
Air Arabia via Sharjah
Air France via Paris
BA from London
Emirates via Dubai
Ethiopian via Addis Ababa
Etihad via Abu Dhabi
Egypt Air via Cairo
Fly Dubai via Dubai
Flynas, a local carrier with links to the Gulf
Jazeera Airways via Kuwait
Kuwait Airlines via Kuwait
Lufthansa via Frankfurt
Middle East Airlines via Jeddah and the Gulf
Oman Air via Muscat
Pegasus via Turkey to Riyadh
Royal Air Maroc via Casablanca
Royal Jordanian via Amman
Salam Air via Muscat
Saudia the national carrier, to Europe, Africa & Asia
Sudan Airways via Khartoum & Port Sudan to Jeddah
Turkish Airlines via Istanbul
Yemenia discontinued at present

This information is subject to change.

Flight disruption around the Muslim world can occur during the Hajj, as planes are used to ferry pilgrims to Jeddah and Makkah.

By sea

There is a ferry service between Jeddah and Port Sudan/Suakin in Sudan. A few foreign overlanders have used this route in the distant past. Try the following company in Jeddah:

Namma Shipping Lines
Head Office: Tel: +966-2-648 7203, Toll free: 920003232
Fax: +966-2-648 7237
Email: amajid@nesma.com
Address: 5th Floor, Hotel Jeddah Trident, Port Road, Hindhavia area.

Their office is south of Al Balad on Hail Street, four blocks south of the intersection with King Fahd street on the east side. They currently sail once a week to Suakin in Sudan on Saturday, and on Thursday from Sudan to Saudi. The service takes 12hrs and normally departs around 7am–8am. Tickets for a car are from $200 plus $80 per person. 1st class cabins start from $20 and should be available once onboard. Take enough water and snacks for the trip, as comforts on board are said to be nothing to talk about – well, maybe a lot to talk about! Other services offered by Namma Shipping are between Jeddah and Suez, and Yanbu to Safarga in Egypt.

Overland routes to Saudi Arabia

Although Saudi Arabia has land borders with Jordan, Iraq, Kuwait, Bahrain, Qatar, the United Arab Emirates, Oman and Yemen, crossing a land border with an e-visa is so far only permitted from Bahrain and the UAE. Check for updates.
www.saudiarabiavisa.com/entry-points-for-tourists

By bus

SAPTCO operates services from Jordan, UAE, Bahrain and Yemen.

Travel within Saudi Arabia

Domestic airlines

Saudia, the national carrier, flies from Riyadh and Jeddah. **Flynas** is another carrier with domestic and international flights. Check also **Flyadeal** to Riyadh, Jeddah, Dammam and Madinah, plus **Nesma Airlines** (www.nesmaairlines.com)

Intercity buses

Regular daily intercity buses run between the main cities – Jeddah, Riyadh, Buraydah, Ha'il, Al Jawf, Tabuk, Dammam, Abha, Jizan and Najran – plus those forbidden to non-Muslims, Madinah and Makkah. They are operated by SAPTCO, www.saptco.com.sa but the website does not seem to work from outside the country thus far.

There are not many buses, because migrant workers don't seem to move around much. Buses are available to tourists, but passengers will not get much of a view along the way and on arrival will have to take a taxi to find accommodation. See under Jeddah for bus services operated by SAPTCO.

City buses
There are hardly any urban buses apart from in Jeddah and Riyadh.

Train
The services from Jeddah to Makkah and Madinah are off-limits to non-Muslims, leaving the services in the east as the only options: Riyadh to Dammam, and the new northern line to Ha'il and Al Jawf. See details under Riyadh.

Metro
Riyadh metro is expected to start operating in late 2020.

Taxi
Taxis are the most common form of city transport. Prices seem to be negotiable and foreigners can expect to pay over the odds, especially to and from airports. **Careem** and **Uber** are also used. In Jeddah no regular taxis operate out of the New Terminal 1 yet. There is a desk run by Lemo Safwa where prices are fixed, except for tips. It's SR65 to the Garden Palace Hotel, one of the closest hotels to the North Terminal. A taxi from this hotel to the North Terminal is SR50–60 early morning. A taxi from the North Terminal to the Red Sea Palace Hotel at Al Balad cost upwards of SR100 (from ticket counters).

Car hire and driving
A car offers so much freedom and saves hours, even though the driving times between towns and sights is massive; we drove over 4500km. That said, driving around Saudi Arabia is no walk in the park. Getting to many places of interest in the country is extremely time-consuming and limited by the SAPTCO buses. Most travellers (ie 2 others we met on our first trip) arriving so far have hired cars from one of the international firms, picking up the vehicle at Jeddah airport. Do take the added extra full insurance for peace of mind.

Car hire in Jeddah
There are three terminals at Jeddah airport; the new Saudi airlines one has the main international car desks. The North Terminal has Budget but no others of international note. The South Terminal has many local companies, but maybe these should be avoided as they speak less English. A yellow shuttle bus runs from the South Terminal to New Terminal 1 for SR20 each. It may be refunded by your car hire company on receipt of the ticket, so don't pay for an expensive taxi. Enterprise has a friendly airport service in English. Book from outside the country for the best deals, with the usual agencies like Expedia/Rental Cars etc offering greater protection.

The local agent for Enterprise/Alamo/National is AJAR (Al Jomaih Auto Rentals). We had excellent service throughout.

Our Land Rover in the northern desert 1974

Hiring a car was a great way to see the country in 2019 & 2020

Car hire in Riyadh

Things are similar when hiring a car from Riyadh airport. The desks are in Terminal 1. There are also cubicles on level 2 of the carpark area across from the terminal and accessed a floor below the main desks and then up on level 2. Enterprise had one here at zone 204. However, on arrival we were taken by car to the Saudia Terminal Five office to complete all the paperwork. It is strongly recommended to get the additional Full Insurance cover. It's a busy office and most cars are kept here. Otherwise it's all straightforward, with passport, visa and driving licence required, plus the credit card deposit of around SR500. (The car was returned to the Terminal 1 / 2 area afterwards.) When driving out of the airport, follow the exit signs from here and be sure to watch **very carefully** if taking the King Salman West Ring Road as the signposting is confusing and the traffic manic. Be sure to get fuel as soon as possible, as most cars are not filled up already.

Given a choice, it's probably marginally easier to hire a car in Jeddah in terms of 'learning to drive' in the country. Riyadh is a massive city with an incredible maze of motorways and city roads and the airport is well to the north. This is fine for a quick getaway directly to the north, but going to the south means horrendous traffic issues for 40km either through the middle of the city or on the western ring road. All routes are congested, especially with the disruption of the new metro construction, which will make driving especially difficult for months to come.

Driving hints

If you thought the M25 in the UK, Italian motorways or India were hectic, think again! At least in India most vehicles can't go very fast. Driving in the large towns of Saudi Arabia is frankly quite harrowing at times. Trying to navigate around them with impatient drivers on all sides needs concentration, a cool head and ideally big mirrors and a loud horn, although there will rarely be time to blow it! Almost no one uses indicators, so expect anything to happen. Avoid the right-hand lanes if going straight ahead at traffic lights; that lane is used by those turning right who don't normally need to stop for the lights to go green! The roads are not busy at all in the desert regions and it's really quite remote in some areas. Beware of cars coming up from behind at colossal speeds. Driver get very close behind; watch in the mirrors for those speeding up the right-hand side anywhere. The dual carriageway roads often have barriers down the middle, which means endless extra kilometres waiting to do a U-turn to get across a road to a turnoff, hotel or café. Beware at roundabouts, as it's unclear who gives way – we think those coming on have right of way, but then again...

Across the country fuel stations are not found for long stretches, so keep the tank filled up. Keep a stock of **food** and **water** in case of delays in the desert. Ideally have a **sleeping bag**, as the nights get bitter in the desert in winter, especially north of Madinah.

All cars seem to be petrol and automatic. Petrol costs SR150–156 (91 grade) per litre. Higher grade (95) petrol is SR205–210. Diesel is available for trucks and cars; it costs from SR0.47 per litre.

Taking a vehicle from Europe

It is also possible to enter Saudi Arabia from the UAE for those with a left-hand drive vehicle of their own. A Carnet de Passage is required. The route from Europe is via Turkey, Iran and then by ferry to UAE from Bandar Abbas in Iran. Exit might be possible from Jordan; keep an eye on this possibility soon. Of course, Syria is in the way at the moment. We met a German couple at Diriyah with their own Toyota 4X4 Camper and three other overlanders in Al Ula.

Finding the way

With a lack of up-to-date detailed printed road maps, the only way to find the way around is with maps.me or Google maps. **Google maps** and **Maps.me** are vital for finding the way in towns and cities, as there are no road signs and only seconds to make a choice with drivers blasting around at high speed on both sides. At least when you inevitably go the wrong way, you will be able to find your way back on track again.

These websites are also not bad for finding accommodation and eateries. Download the maps to your phone or device while on Wi-Fi at home or in your hotel; most hotels have Wi-Fi. Some car hire companies provide SatNav for a daily fee, but we managed OK with a smart phone and these two apps.

Road survival kit

For any road journey, be sure to have emergency food and water; there are long distances between service stations and some of these don't have food. Some of those that do look rather insalubrious, with flies getting a first go at the food on offer. The following is a suggested survival list for Saudi Arabia. A kettle is really vital to get drinks, as hotels rarely offer any cafés, food or drinks. A thermos is great for refreshment in the desert.

Sleeping bags are a must for those contemplating periods (camping or in rough accommodation) in the desert, as it gets incredibly cold. Some hotels may supply a suite of several rooms, but no sheets or towels, so that's another reason to be well equipped.

Road survival kit
The following list is a guideline for drivers and travellers. Some will need to be brought from home, but food supplies can be bought in local supermarkets.

Electric kettle	Muesli
Filter for water	Bread
Multi-adaptor for electric sockets	Tin of fish
Mug	Cheese
Knife, spoon, penknife	Peanut butter
Bowl	Instant mashed potato
Thermos flask	Tea, coffee, sugar, etc
Towel & toiletries	Milk powder/yoghurt

Tour operators
Some visitors to Saudi Arabia are about to begin travelling on trips organised by the few foreign tour operators interested. The local tour operators have a limited offering and selections, mainly for weekends and day trips. Independent travel is perfectly possible and the most common way to visit so far. See list of tour operators in Appendix 5.

Visa information

Saudi Arabia visa www.saudiarabiavisa.com

The country has recently introduced a tourist e-visa system after years of being closed to travellers. Obtaining the e-visa is relatively simple online, although the form-filling takes some time. A multiple entry visa costs around SAR464 (just under £100) for British citizens, including compulsory emergency travel insurance. So long as the application form is filled in correctly, the visa might be issued within a few minutes or three days. Visas are NOT available on arrival.

The new e-visa offers entry through four airports and two land borders, from Bahrain and the UAE, but not yet the road from Jordan. Other entry points are being developed to accommodate e-visa arrivals in future. Passports should be valid for six months at the time of travel. The visa is valid for one year, with each visit up to 90 days. **Please check the website to confirm details.**

Jordan visa
Visas can be obtained on arrival by many nationalities and are sometimes free of cost if travelling on a tour with a Jordanian agency. Do check online or with your local Jordanian embassy in case of any changes.

UAE visa
Many nationals do not require a visa to enter the country. Check before any travel plans are finalised.

Oman visa
The e-visa for Oman is available online. Check at www.omanvisaonline.org

Kuwait visa
The e-visa for Kuwait is available online. Some nationalities can get a visa on arrival. Check at www.evisa.moi.gov.kw

Bahrain visa
Visas are available on arrival and may require proof of a ticket to leave the country.

Qatar
The on-going issues between the Gulf communities and Qatar had not been resolved at the time of publication.

Money matters

> I now add worry about the cash supply to my collection of other possible misfortunes.
> *Stones of Silence*, **George Schaller**

The currency is the Saudi Riyal (SAR/SR). Notes come in the following denominations: 500, 200, 100, 50, 10, 5 and 1 notes, with some smaller coins SR2 and SR1 as well. Some people refuse torn notes – beware! It is currently pegged to the US$ at US$1 = SR3.75.

Approximate exchange rates (March 2020)	
	SAR
£	4.89
€	4.23
US$	3.75
CHF	3.99

There are ATMs across the country, although far fewer outside the main towns. Look for the Al Rajhi and NCB bank machines. There are virtually no exchange bureaux anywhere, so be sure to have a credit/debit card. It might be possible to exchange cash at the occasional 'Quick Pay' offices normally used by migrant workers to send money home, but we do not have any experience of this. Some people may accept payment in US$, since the rate is currently fixed.

Take a bit more local cash (and US Dollars) than you think you will need when in the rural areas. Riyals must be normally used for fuel, cafés and hotels. Foreign credit cards are not popular outside of big centres. It's best to have sufficient cash riyals; you can change any surplus back at the airport on departure.

Language
The main language of Saudi Arabia is of course Arabic, with English understood by some. English is taught in schools across the country and understood to varying extents by all staff involved in tourism.

Internet and phone
A full range of internet-based services are available across the country. The international dialling code is **+966.**

Mobile phones have completely changed the nature of 'getting away from it all' anywhere these days and in Saudi it is the same. 5G is available in the larger cities. Wi-Fi is almost everywhere. It's no big deal to call anywhere across the globe from a desert oasis.

Nowadays people in the smallest village can keep in touch with family. However, there are a few isolated corners of the country where mobile coverage is absent or erratic, so try not to break a leg! Services may suffer issues near the borders.

Electricity
Electricity in the country is generally 220V/60Hz, but it some places it is 110V; the vast majority of sockets are three-pin British style, but some are round two-pin European style, and very occasionally flat two-pin sockets are found. Electrification covers the whole country, bar a few isolated places. Charging your camera battery and computer is easy, but be sure to bring an electrical adaptor as well as more spare batteries than you expect to use.

National holidays

The following are some of the main holidays. Other holidays may occur regionally.

Public Holidays	
Jan 01	New Year's Day
May 01	Labour Day
May 25	Resistance and Liberation Day
Sep 01	Hijri New Year
Sep 10	Ashoura
Nov 10	Birthday of Prophet Muhammad (pbuh)
Nov 22	Independence Day
Varying dates	Eid el Fitr (end of Ramadan, varies)

Some other dates and holidays also vary.

Trip planning

Permits

Travel permits are not required anywhere on the roads, although restrictions could be imposed on the border areas, as one might expect. Independent travellers should steer well clear of military areas near the borders. This might apply to Najran near the Yemeni border at times, and it does seem to apply to the Iraqi border zone.

Permits are required for some **archaeological sites**. In theory it should be possible to contact the Dept of Antiquities in Riyadh, but there is no listed email. Otherwise try the tourist hotline on 930 for help once in the country or DGDA – https://dgda.gov.sa; email: info@dgda.gov.sa; tel: 92 000 26 22. Address: 7747 Umro adhamry Street-Diplomatic Quarter Unit 2#, Riyadh 12512

National parks/reserves

Visitors to most of the mountain areas are not currently charged any fees. Do check for any changes, though. There are some designated national parks, and permits are required for some. The Saudi Wildlife Authority (SWA) controls the parks, with an office in southwest Riyadh, between Al Fikr Street and Almam Abdul Aziz ibn Muhammad ibn Saud – www.swa.gov.sa; info@swa.gov.sa

Choosing the season

The best season for travel to Saudi Arabia is during the northern winter between late October/November and before April when the temperatures soar to 40°C and even higher. The mountains of the southwest have a longer season, due to the ameliorating effects of the higher altitudes. Here the season could be between October and late April. Sandstorms can be an issue in spring, as the weather turns in March/April.

Maps

> Frodo began to feel restless, and the old paths seemed too well-trodden. He looked at maps and wondered what lay beyond their edges: maps made in the Shire showed mostly white spaces beyond its borders.
> ***The Lord of the Rings*, J R R Tolkien**

There are not many printed maps of Saudi Arabia, and most of those still available date back to 2009 and earlier. Roads are being built at such a pace that these maps can only be used for outline planning.

Map of Saudi Arabia ITMB 2004
Saudi Arabia (including Iran, Iraq, Kuwait, Jordan, Bahrain, UAE, Oman, Yemen, Qatar) Road Map Freytag & Berndt, Apr 2005
Saudi Arabien Reise Know-How Verlag 14 Jan 2009
Africa North East, Arabia 745 Michelin 2019

Stanfords (www.stanfords.co.uk)
The Map Centre (www.themapcentre.com)
The Map Shop (www.themapshop.co.uk)

Photography

The variety of the subject matter is mind-boggling. The mountains and the coast are glorious in all their colourful aspects. The vibrant people, bustling markets, architecture, antiquities and natural scenery offer wonderful opportunities. Some will find interest in the astonishing modernist buildings of Riyadh. Ideally keep your photographic equipment in plastic bags, away from the unavoidable dust, especially across the desert areas. Bring cleaning equipment. Opportunities to recharge batteries are easily found except in the desert areas, although a two- or three-pin (UK) plug adaptor may be necessary. It's best to pack extra batteries and memory cards.

Avoid taking photographs of any military-looking subjects, such as checkposts, bridges and communication towers. You are strongly urged to ask permission of people (particularly women) before taking photographs, especially in the conservative areas. Taking pictures around military areas is not a good idea. **Ask** at all times if in doubt or taking a forbidden picture might need a long visa extension!

Budgeting

Saudi Arabia is not necessarily an expensive destination, although it's is easy to rack up big bills using local tour agents. Hotels and food are quite reasonable. Some hotels can be as expensive as many in Western Europe, but there is a wide range of less expensive places.

Food in the shops and supermarkets is good value, but the restaurants (where found) are also quite pricey, especially in luxury hotels. A buffet lunch in a 4* hotel could run to SR75–100 ($25) plus. Hummus in such a place with bread is OK for SR15–25. A cappuccino in a good café in Jeddah might cost SR15. Elsewhere perhaps SR8–10.

As for transport, the SAPTCO buses are not so expensive considering the distances involved between cities. Jeddah to Madinah is US$32 for example, although buying a ticket as a foreigner might become difficult. Currently all that is needed is the cash. The SAPTCO buses are modern and comfortable.

A taxi from Jeddah airport into the centre might cost SR100–150 on arrival, but getting around the city is much cheaper.

Costs

Top class hotels are expensive (SR700–2500), especially in Al Ula during the festival. Mid-range are around SR250–400 and the vast majority of apartment-style places are from SR100–150. A fast-food takeaway meal might cost SR12–15 per person and in a good hotel restaurant a lot more, say SR40–100; alcohol is not available. Bottled water in a shop costs SR3 for 1½ltr, SR5 for 5ltr. Greek-style yoghurt SR3. Tea/coffee in a hotel, SR10–15. For those with hired cars or with their own wheels, the cost of fuel is: Petrol SR1.50–1.56 and Diesel SR0.47 per litre.

Accommodation

Apart from in the large cities, very few hotels are marked in English. This makes finding places to stay a real issue for tourists. There are a few tell-tale signs that a building is a hotel; most display bright neon lights, are above shops, have many AC boxes and an entry door into a small reception area at street level. Other good indicators are the fire escape stairways outside, mostly made of metal.

Some hotels/motels are found above the shops of bigger fuel stations. This is a good option for drivers, as there is no parking issue and less traffic to deal with outside of the towns. Many are not so smart though. Most so-called hotels are apartment-style for families, meaning a couple or more bedrooms plus bathroom, lounge and small basic kitchen. Expect hotels, especially those classified as apartments, to be rudderless during afternoon prayers and until 4pm, when receptions are more likely to be open.

Big city hotels are expensive, often 5 star and internationally recognisable. Mid-range places can cost from SR250–400 and much more. Budget hotels start from SR80–120 or so upwards to SR150.

A hotel at a fuel station in Shigry

Eating out and food

Restaurants are found in all the big cities but, surprisingly outside of these, the choice is much more limited. Fast-food outlets are everywhere but having chicken nuggets and chips every day might get boring. In the smaller towns these places can shut early (6pm), while others do not open until 6pm. Very confusing! Other eateries if you can find them seem to open later, but each town seems to be different, and at weekends more places might be open. The Al Baik chain is a popular fast-food chicken and chips joint all over the country.

Restaurant in the Hotel Azd, Abha

Where the food is local-style, in say hotel restaurants, the food is wholesome and great. All those tasty dishes like hummus, kebabs and salads etc are normally available at lunch and dinner in posh places. The black bean dish, foul medames, is only eaten for breakfast. Elsewhere in the truck stops, the food doesn't look very appetising. Luckily flat bread comes with almost every dish, so there's no need to go hungry anywhere.

Local fast food offerings

Bananas and bread with cream cheese triangles from a supermarket might get to be a daily staple in the wilder areas. The local coffee is different, served in small cups and made with green beans and ginger. Tea/chai comes in small glasses. Cafés at the better fuel stations often have an OK choice around midday, when intercity buses might drop by.

The supermarkets have quite a varied choice of food for emergencies, like tins of foul (beans) or fish, biscuits, imported cheese, bread and cakes in sealed bags for longer life, and chocolate.

Those wishing to camp (if trekking for example) can buy small and large gas supplies but finding them is quite difficult. Try the larger supermarkets at fuel stations. We noted a great supply at Shigry, probably for those wanting to explore the Shaq Canyon. Sun Gas in smaller cans seems the best choice for the odd night of camping. They appear to cost SR90–100.

Tipping
For those on organised trips and those who have received good service, tipping is tricky, since it depends on the group size and number of staff. We have no real idea about income levels and tipping, but your tour guide may be able to give some pointers. Elsewhere, apart from big hotels, tipping is not common, it seems.

Style of trip
As much as anything, the itinerary you choose and the destinations to be visited will dictate the style of trip.

Independent trips

Going independently is quite a challenge as the country is not really geared up for such visitors. That said, the expat communities have been travelling around the country for years in a limited way.

This form of travel does allow for perhaps greater interaction and a close rapport with the inhabitants who can speak English. It is also much cheaper than any group arrangement. That said, there is an element of time-wasting – either learning where to catch the bus, or getting lost in one-way systems and waiting to do a U-turn on a motorway. Getting side-tracked by information that seems wide of the mark seems to happen, though not out of malice. Ask more than one person if unsure; after all, not many Saudis travel around their own country that much.

Independently organised trips

When the Saudi authorities suddenly began issuing e-visas, did anyone expect to be able to arrive and just take off for any and all destinations? In fact we arrived not knowing for sure if we could go anywhere much, whether by taking a local bus or hiring a car. In the event we hired a car online in advance in hope, and so did two other parties we met at the Al Ula winter festival – the only other tourists we met in the whole country. Thus far there do not seem to be any restrictions on where to go. The only possible restriction might be the far south near Yemen and also near the Iraq border.

It's perfectly possible to approach a local tour operator to organise a trip in Saudi Arabia, although so far most of the trips on offer are day excursions. That is quite restricting and very expensive. A few agents can organise a few days in the Empty Quarter from Riyadh. More trips of longer duration are sure to come on stream soon. When agents will organise trekking trips is anyone's guess. Some areas of the desert would have great appeal and maybe the mountains around Abha, although security issues are an issue in the far south.

Opening a door on a mysterious country

Fully organised group trips

For those with limited time, this option provides maximum security and the least amount of hassle. The overseas tour operators can smooth over any local difficulties and sort out transport, smoothing away the delays of local buses and obtaining any special permits necessary. They can also help with visas for those nationalities that may need them.

All day-to-day logistics such as accommodation, food, transport and carriage of baggage will be arranged. Most trips are fully inclusive, with few added extras. Clients can admire the archaeological sites and scenery in as much comfort as is possible.

The 'Rawi' – storyteller – guides of Al Ula are friendly, informative and very enthusiastic.

Ask permission before taking such photos.

There are a few disadvantages to commercial group trips. Naturally all these services cost a lot more money. The major problem is that there is a loss of flexibility concerning the itinerary and any other issues. There is always the risk that your fellow travellers are on a different planet – although this is extremely rare. Saudi Arabia, for some, is already on another planet!

Guides and drivers

Group trips will be led by a local leader/guide/driver who knows the routes. Most European groups will have a European leader for the first few seasons as tourism develops.

What to take for a trek

The following list is a guideline only and applies to those considering a desert or mountain trek:

Kitbag	Walking poles
Torch (flashlight) & whistle	Trainers or sandals
Washing kit	Fleece and woollen hat
Wetwipes, large and small	Sunglasses & sun hat
Toothbrush & toothpaste	Gloves and scarf/buff
Sun cream & lip cream	Waterproof jacket/trousers
Water bottle	Warm sweater
Trousers or cotton skirts	Down jacket/trousers
Shirts, T-shirts or blouses	Penknife and tin opener
Underwear	Padlock for cheap hotel
Boots and various socks	rooms
Sleeping bag + fleece liner	Ear plugs
Toilet rolls	Camera & batteries
Plastic bags	Adaptor for electric plugs

Staying healthy

The main problems concerning health issues are limited to bad luck in the main and related to food, water, hygiene and, for a few in future, the remoteness of the desert and mountain areas. Since Bob's first visit in 1974, the food and hygiene scene has changed radically. Personal hygiene and what you eat still matter, but today most reputable restaurants and cafés are excellent.

Do your best to keep healthy
Wash/clean hands regularly
Never drink untreated tap water
Salads are a risk if washed in unclean water
Peel fruits
Brush teeth in bottled/cleaned water

Saudi Arabia has some very well qualified medical personnel, should the worst happen. Outside the main centres there are fewer medical facilities. If necessary, try asking at Nahdi and Al Dawaa pharmacies.

Be sure to get adequate insurance cover for the trip, even though local emergency medical insurance is included in the visa application. That said, all the usual basic rules of travelling abroad still apply.

Water sterilisation

Tap water in parts of Saudi Arabia is not considered safe to drink without boiling. In the mountain areas, locals claim that springs are in good shape, but visitors may not be used to the minerals in the water. Bottled drinking water is available from most corner stores and would seem to be pretty safe. Of course plastic water bottles do create unwanted litter, so be sure to dispose of them appropriately. Adding sterilising tablets is another way around the issue of bad water. Iodine or chlorine tablets, or Micropur, can be used.

> **See also www.watertogo.eu and get a
> 15% discount using the code SB15**

Antibacterial gel for hands and large baby wipes for other parts are extremely useful! Bring plastic bags for storing used items and deal with rubbish appropriately in the hills.

Vaccinations

Your GP can advise you about the latest recommendations regarding vaccinations. Be sure to allow plenty of time for the series of vaccinations – they cannot all be given at the same time and some require several weeks in-between. Keep a record of all the vaccinations, even though most are not a legal requirement.

The following are normally recommended by health professionals, but others could be added at any time.

BCG tuberculosis Vaccination is often recommended by GPs.
Cholera Although not required by law or particularly effective, it might be recommended if an outbreak has occurred.
Hepatitis This nasty disease has various forms; hepatitis A is the main risk for travellers. New vaccines are being improved for all strains of hepatitis.
Meningitis Outbreaks do occur in rural parts, but the risk is minimal and expensive vaccines are available.
Rabies There is a small risk of rabies in the rural areas where dogs are used for guarding property, although most are well looked after by their owners. Beware of the troops of **monkeys** on routes in the mountains of the Asir. The vaccination is expensive and the

procedure lengthy. Casual visitors should keep a sharp lookout for suspiciously acting dogs.

Tetanus/polio Recommended.

Typhoid/paratyphoid Vaccinations are strongly recommended, as there are possible risks.

Other nasty bugs

Giardia is a wretched bug to watch out for, since there is no preventative treatment apart from careful eating and drinking. Infected drinking water is the main culprit. Giardia lives happily in its host until sent packing by a course of Flagyl (Metronidazole), Secnidazole or Tinidazole. Sulphurous foul-smelling gases, cramp and sometimes diarrhoea are the main symptoms, but let's not dwell on those.

Dengue fever outbreaks are sometimes reported in Africa, but the risk is generally fairly low in Saudi Arabia. Try to avoid mosquito bites, since there is no treatment other than rest.

Malaria

Fortunately malaria is not generally found in the desert regions of the country. The coastal regions of the Red Sea and the Gulf may have risks. Be sure to ask your doctor, since cases do occur in nearby Egypt.

Using insect repellent at and after dusk and wearing suitable clothing will give some protection against bites. The three main drugs used are Doxycycline, Malarone (Atovaquone/proguanil) and Mefloquine (Lariam). Lariam has effectively been dumped since the side effects are rather dire for many people.

Always check with health professionals before embarking on a trip, in case the advice has changed.

Common ailments

The most common problems are colds, coughs, blocked sinuses, headaches and stomach disorders. Common remedies (available from the chemist) for headaches, blocked noses, sore throats, coughs and sneezes should be easily accessible in any medical kit. Take a good supply of decongestants and painkillers for headaches. It is necessary to drink more liquids in the dry regions.

If the dreaded stomach bug appears, the use of Imodium, Loperamide or Lomotil is initially recommended if symptoms are not serious. These drugs will make a road journey much more comfortable. The antibiotic drugs Norfloxacin and Ciprofloxacin can be used in more debilitating cases.

Dioralyte will help rehydration in cases of fluid loss due to stomach upsets. Stemetil can be used for those prone to travel sickness.

It may seem obvious, but don't ignore the power of the sun. Wear a suitable hat and cover your arms and legs; use sun cream on exposed parts of the body.

Dental care
A visit to your dentist for a check-up before the trip is advised. Competent dentists exist in Saudi Arabia at a price, so make sure your insurance covers this issue.

First aid kit

The following list is only given as a suggestion:

Antibacterial hand gel	Insect repellent
Antibiotics (general)	Knee bandage
Antihistamine cream	Safety pins
Antiseptic cream	Scissors
Aspirin/paracetamol	Sterile gloves
Blister prevention	Sun cream
Rehydration sachets	Thermometer
Dressings	Water sterilising tablets
Eyewash	Wet wipes

Plus: Pocket First Aid and Wilderness Medicine
Dr Jim Duff and Dr Peter Gormly (Cicerone)
Cold and sinus remedies
Personal medications
Stomach upset remedies and Tinidazole

If this lot fails to sort you out, check out the local remedies.

Clinics
Consult one of the specialist clinics or their websites listed below for the latest medical advice for travellers. Your doctor should also be consulted.

International Society of Travel Medicine www.istm.org
Hospital for Tropical Diseases Travel Clinic www.thehtd.org
MASTA (Medical Advisory Service for Travellers Abroad) www.masta-travel-health.com

> Before there were tourists there were travellers, before them explorers, and before them all, traders and pilgrims.
> *Arabia Deserta*, **Charles M Doughty 1888**

General safety

The biggest issue in Saudi Arabia come from the high temperatures. Unnoticed dehydration is easily overlooked; you may not necessarily feel like drinking – remember that tea and coffee are both diuretics, so keep vital fluids up. Electrolyte powders can be added to clean water if lethargy arises (apart from when going up steep trails, when a little tiredness can easily be explained!). Noting the colour of your urine is one good way to be aware of dehydration. If it's very yellow, you are not drinking enough. Breathing through a scarf when exercising heavily can help to retain fluids and will help protect against dust and draining winds. The locals, male and female, learned long ago to cover up.

Always concentrate and take care during any walking or longer trekking. Leaping carelessly across boulders or soft soils and sands is an easy way to fall foul of snags. Be careful exploring those fabulous outcrops – it's easy to get carried away with the novelty and excitement of discovering dark canyons and narrow ravines. Be aware that scorpions lurk in shady spots.

Unruly dogs are a definite issue in the high areas where farmers use them to guard and control livestock in the hills. However, near a village, during a night-time visit to the toilet if camping, watch out! The monkeys in the Asir may be cute, but they can be very aggressive and will jump at cars in search of morsels. Beware!

There is no need to be put off by all the above advice; just take care and enjoy the trip!

Weather

In general the country is hot, with a limited cool season from the end of October to March. Remember the highest mountains may have snow a few times in mid-winter. Sandstorms seem more frequent in the spring, beginning early March.

Security

The culture of the desert Arabs was to give shelter to a fellow traveller, and to a degree this still applies in the wild areas. Those days for the most part have long gone, and today every government is issuing so many warnings that it is a surprise that anyone goes anywhere, even Bognor (UK joke)! Saudi Arabia has long been considered a safe country in general. A few violent incidents have occurred in the past, but not recently. Such things are likely anywhere across the globe now.

That is not to say an incident can be ruled out. Anyone wanting to visit Saudi Arabia should be prepared to **take full responsibility** for their visit and not expect any help from outside agencies. Independent travellers may feel slightly uncomfortable where few ever venture. Foreigners should not get too close to the Yemeni border and may also experience a mixed reception in ultra-conservative areas.

Using this guide

The following details appertained at the time of our visit, but of course things change from time to time. We have not endeavoured to list all the accommodation options, since these are readily available on hotel booking websites. Route descriptions indicate approximate distances, timings and altitudes where relevant.

The limited itineraries shown in the appendix summaries reflect the possible routes and durations. We have listed the main places of interest and what to see across the country. Being such a vast country, it is not possible to visit all the possible places of note, especially as the country has literally just opened to tourism.

Pre-travel checklist
Ideally don't travel alone in Saudi Arabia, especially in the mountains.
Register your journey with your embassy (if travelling independently).
Make sure you have adequate insurance.
Carry a photocopy of your passport and visa details page.
Carry a first aid kit and medications.
Treat local staff properly.
Respect the culture, the environment and local sensibilities.
Dress appropriately.
Watch your step in the hills!

This car in Jeddah ain't going anywhere!

The motto for explorers and visitors around the world is:
'Leave only footprints and take only photographs'
Enjoy your trip!

EXPLORING SAUDI ARABIA

It is not the goal but the way there that matters, and the harder the way the more worthwhile the journey.
Wilfred Thesiger

Saudi Arabia 1974
Bob first visited the country in 1974, while driving overland to Kathmandu. In Beirut they obtained Saudi transit visas to reach the Gulf and routes to the east. In those days getting a transit visa for Saudi Arabia was possible, although it was a rather hit-and-miss affair. The road was excellent across the country even then, with sealed highways from Aqaba in Jordan, via Tabuk and Khaybar to Medina (now Madinah). The usual route was along the so-called Pipeline Highway directly from Jordan to Dammam on the Gulf coast. Their route took them from the Medina ring road to Riyadh for a visa extension, and then east to Dammam and up to Kuwait. It was during July and incredibly hot, although perhaps not as hot as today. Some of the pictures in this guide reflect the period.

Jeddah – one gateway to Saudi Arabia

Introduction
Riyadh would normally be the most likely gateway to Saudi Arabia, but due to the multitude of sights in the western region of the country, many are likely to fly into Jeddah (also spelt Jiddah). It's a large city some 30-40km across and is the main port for the Red Sea coast. The melting pot of inhabitants is amazing: Eritreans, Somalis, Sudanese, Egyptians, Indians, Pakistanis, Bangladeshis and others rub shoulders with local Saudis. The old city Al Balad and souk are about as traditional as anyone will find in the country. It's a great window on the country.

Getting into town
The large airport is around 25km from the central areas and, for simplicity, taking a taxi is the easiest option. Of course, it's not the cheapest choice. From the North Terminal there are large minivan-style taxis for 7–10 people, but if only 2 it still costs SR100 with a ticket bought inside the terminal from a counter after customs (some taxi drivers will ask for more even with this ticket!). There are three money exchange places here as well, and rates are normally the same as in town. Finding a bus into town from this terminal seems impossible. The urban SAPTCO bus system is absent here. The impressive Hajj terminal is to the north of the North Terminal.

Finding a bus would serve the purposes of cost effectiveness, but it's a large city to find one's way around as a stranger. Theoretically a SAPTCO bus costs US$1–3, but there was no sign of it. The traffic means it can take 1hr to town. Buses do not seem to run on Sundays, even if they do at other times.

Exchanging cash US$ is not that easy around town even in banks, it seems, so get enough at the airport for immediate needs. Banks might only want US$100 bills! ATMs are found at the Al Rajhi Bank and UCB bank near Makkah Gate. Apparently if desperate there are a few exchange places are in the old city near Makkah Gate, but we did not find any.

Transport options
The main SAPTCO Intercity station with proper ticket offices is on Ha'il street. There is a manned kiosk in the ticket office; some English is spoken. Sample routes and times for Monday morning:

From Jeddah to:		Time taken
Madinah	09.05	4hrs 50mins
Jizan	09.59	12hrs
Riyadh	10.00	11hrs 30mins
Najran	10.30	14hrs 10mins
Makkah	10.30	1hr 25mins; No non-Muslims
Tabuk	10.30	14hrs
Sana'a	11.00	26hrs really, it's listed!!
Madinah	11.00	4hrs 50mins
Makkah	12.00	1hr 25mins
Riyadh	12.00	13hrs 30mins

Buses to:
Riyadh: every 2–3 hours, costing SR173–184
Tabuk: every 2–3 hours, costing SR179 via the Red Sea coast
Abha: every 2–3hrs, costing SR137 (8–9hrs)
Madinah: costs SR120 and stops outside the Haram area
Al Ula: infrequent via Tabuk, so need to ask specifically. Tabuk to Al Ula takes 4hrs.

City buses
There are hardly any town buses apart from in Jeddah.
Private buses run take pilgrims to Makkah from the large parking area to the north of SAPTCO, but tourists cannot use these.

Getting around the city there are red SAPTCO bus services but getting the right one is tricky. Bus 9 and 10 head to the Al Balad (old city) bus stop on the road parallel to Ha'il street to the east.

The ferry to Sudan is located southwest of the old city area.

Accommodation

There is a wide range of mostly good hotels; prices are not prohibitive except for the posh places. The Red Sea Palace on the waterfront near the old souk area Al Balad is a great place to start with; although not at the cheaper end, it is comfortable and conveniently located (from SR215 upwards depending on the season). Check it out at reservations@menaredseapalace.com or on booking.com. Nearby and also convenient for the old city is the Albaia Hotel, reservations@albaiahotel.com (SR200–220). The Indian Oyo chain has a few places across the city. Check the usual well-known websites. Near the North Terminal on the west side is the Garden Palace Hotel about 4km from the airport, if you have an early flight.

Eating

A reasonable meal will cost SR25–40 for anything worth eating. Most hotels have restaurants but are more expensive SR40–75 in a hotel. If you're driving, there are apparently a lot of restaurants, with some good value places among all the posher ones. For tea, coffee and cakes, Café Magad in Al Balad is atmospheric, with some 50-year-old pictures of Jeddah inside, with the various 'legations' and consulates marked, as well the city walls and boundaries. English tea cost SR6, coffee SR10, plus VAT. It's a great place to slump in historic confines.

The sights

There is no printed city map, so you'll have to look at Google or maps.me or similar. Jeddah is a massive city with a lot of modern areas. The main sight is the old city area called Al Balad. Allow two days for a decent exploration of the city.

Old City

As might be expected of a true Arab old city, the Al Balad area is a warren of alleys and lanes with some high-rise traditional houses displaying wonderfully carved wooden windows and doors. The merchant houses and buildings are generally white with brown wooden decorated windows and balconies. Some buildings are painted green, while others are a beautiful shade of blue.

Although the old city does not now have any wall, there are a couple of significant gates. On the north side is the lonely-looking Al Madinah (Al Jadid) Gate. On the east side along the Hajj path is the impressively rebuilt Bab al Makkah in Ottoman style. The central Al Shaf'i mosque (sometimes called the Jami mosque) dates from the 7th century and has an impressive restored minaret. It's not open to foreigners.

Among all the tower houses is the tall Nassif House museum, see below. It was not open during our visits! Elsewhere are a few small local mosques, some old and a couple much bigger new ones.

Be sure to take tea or coffee and cakes at the Café Magad north of the Nassif House museum. Café Madinah is not marked in English and is a more local affair. There are a few snack places, mainly open after 4pm, but no restaurants as such that we found. As for shopping, the best time is in the evenings, when the bazaar wakes up after the heat of the day.

Map of Al Balad, Jeddah old city (not to scale)

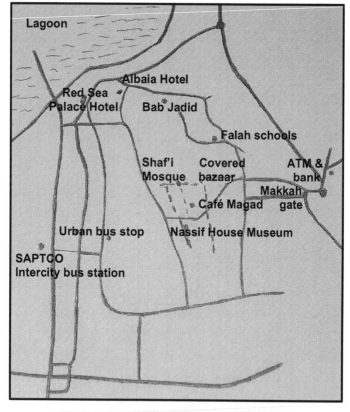

Typical merchant house in Al Balad, old Jeddah

Souks

Animated and colourful, the souk (Suq) is a must-see sight in the old city area. The covered souk is close to Souk Bab Makkah, which leads down to Makkah Gate on the east side of the old city. The covered souk is not a very large area, but it's very colourful and lively after 5pm and in the evenings. The area near Makkah Gate is also a bustling area of fruit sellers and shops. Souk al Jami is adjacent to the Shaf'i mosque near the open area of the Bedouin market and is really a line of shops. Another modern souk is on the west side, but it is less animated.

Museums
The museum of Nassif House (Bayt Naseef) is located in the old city nearer the southern end. Originally built for Omar Nassif Efendi in 1872, it was completed in 1881. The building was used as a residence by Abdul Aziz after the siege of Jeddah in 1925. The house is shaded by a tall tree and is known here as the 'house with the tree'. With over 100 rooms, it could take some time to discover its gems. It opened as a museum in 2009 and once housed thousands of books as a library of Muhammad Naseef. Currently it is not very often open.

Al Tayyebat Museum is located in the Hejazi heritage village and has exhibits about the culture, clothing and way of life across the country.

New Corniche
The best time to visit the Corniche of Al Hamra along the Red Sea is naturally at sunset, when the colours and ambience are at their best. The main zone of the corniche runs from the red Ruwais Mosque to Al Hamra street. The red mosque is an interesting building, but parking around here is tricky with so many one-way roads and long gaps between U-turns. The Red Sea Mall is a stylish place to visit.

Across the waterfront from the old city is a modern area with the white multi-domed Juffali Mosque and high-rise blocks behind. The rest of Jeddah is modern, and many buildings and areas have tastefully designed architecture. The snag is that modern Jeddah covers a vast area and a car is really the only way to get about.

The famous Café Magad in Jeddah

Riyadh – another gateway to Saudi Arabia

Introduction

Riyadh, the capital since the formation of the country in 1932, was a relatively small manageable-sized city even in 1974. That of course has changed radically, as contemporary Riyadh reflects the country, its growing population and modernity. Towering skyscrapers and impressive high-rise structures characterise the city skyline, and wide motorways are the arteries that try to keep it functioning. It's hard to imagine that any historic structures remain here, but a few have survived.

Getting into town

The airport is around 35km north of the city. The international car hire firms are found in Terminal 1–2 and the Rajhi Bank about 100m away. They also have desks at the domestic Terminal 5. Rials are pegged to the US$ at 3.75. There is a tourist information desk at the airport. Taking a taxi to town is the only option at the moment if you don't hire a car. Taxis are found outside and charge SR100 to the central area, or more depending on the location. The new metro, when open, should be less expensive. The Yellow Line is due to operate from Terminal 5 to eight stations, with links to other lines and destinations. It will probably not open before late 2020 or after.

Transport options

The intercity bus station (SAPTCO) is near Hamra Plaza, about 500m from the 'Train Mall'. A taxi will find it more easily than walking. Services link Riyadh with Jeddah, Madinah, Makkah, Tabuk and the Gulf cities. The cost to Jeddah is SR173–184 (Dec 2019).

There are two train line services from Riyadh. The SAR Trains run to Al Majmaah, Al Qasim, Ha'il and Al Jawf (Jauf): www.sar.com.sa. The Saudi Railway Train runs from Riyadh to Al Hufuf, Aqaiq and Dammam: www.saudirailways.org

Getting around the city, there are local bus services run by SAPTCO with routes 7, 8, 9, 10, 16 and 17; they run from the southern area of town south of Al Mansourah near Al Batha, the area served by numbers 7, 8, 10, 16 and 17. Al Rawdah, east of the centre, is served by 10 and the Public Transportation Centre by number 9. Buses don't run that frequently.

In addition, the brand-new metro system mentioned above is due to open in 2021, with six lines, eighty-five stations and almost 200km of track. If this is not enough to get about, there are always taxis to bargain with.

Map of Riyadh (not to scale)

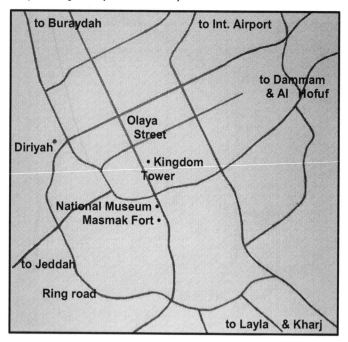

Accommodation

There is a wide range of mostly good hotels and prices are not prohibitive, except for the posh places. Cheaper places can be found from around SR150 upwards on the usual booking websites. We stayed between the National Museum and the high-rise downtown area at Hotel Almakan 105, found on Booking.com. It cost SR406 for 3 nights (dbl) but hot water was pretty elusive. Breakfast cost SR20 per person. The Al Muhaideb nearby is also on Booking.com at SR260 dbl and, if you have the cash, is a much better deal. There is on-going Metro station and road construction around here, but it is within a long walk of the Masmak Fort and the National Museum.

Eating

A reasonable meal will cost SR25–40 for anything worth eating. Most top hotels have restaurants, but they are much more expensive. There are a lot of restaurants, with some good value places among all the posher ones. Fast food has taken over everywhere. The Lulu supermarket in Avenue Mall is close by and has an amazing choice of stuff to buy, as well as its own take-away section. Grilled chicken and chips cost SR10.90. Upstairs are more of the familiar fast food joints. Small gas cookers are found here if required. Cost SR29 plus SR5.30 per cannister.

History

The city of Ar Riyadh was originally called Hajar in the province known then as Al Yamama. At that time the scattered settlement was inhabited by the tribes of Tasam and Jardeis. The city is located above a number of wadis that surround the area of the greater Najd region. In the 5th century AD it was ruled by Obeid bin Ta'laba, the most prominent of the Al Yamama dynasties of the Bani Hanifa. The city, although small, became wealthy from trade.

The walls of Riyadh were rebuilt in 1704 by Dham bin Dwas and later added to by Imam Turki bin Abdullah I in 1823. A few years earlier in 1818 the Turks had destroyed Diriyah and made Riyadh their capital. In 1862 the traveller William Palgrave visit Riyadh during the reign of Imam Faysal bin Turki and recorded many aspects of the city. He later published his findings in a book, Narrative of a Journey through Central and Eastern Arabia.

The Al Rashid clans held Riyadh from 1881 and they trashed the walls in 1891. The city was regained by Abdul Aziz Al Saud after his conquest of Riyadh in 1902. Henceforth Riyadh remained the city of the Al Saud, being proclaimed the capital by Abdul Aziz in 1932 after the country was unified.

Since the early seventies the city has grown at around 8% annually to become the giant that it is today.

Overheating in Riyadh 1974 – personal history

The sights

There aren't any obvious old-fashioned city maps available, although there is one outline simple map in some hotels. Better to use the usual internet map sites and be looking at a small screen all day! Allow two days for a decent exploration of the city and sites like Diriyah close by. Hidden away below the modern city there are a few historic areas to explore.

Riyadh, the water tower in 1974

Riyadh, the water tower in 2020

Al Masmak Fort and museum

The impressive Al Masmak Fort is a highlight of Riyadh and not to be missed. Abdul-Aziz al Saud returned from exile in Kuwait in 1902 to capture the fort from the Al Rashid clan under Ajlan bin Muhammad bin Ajlan, commander of the garrison at the fortress. From that time the al Saud gained power and established Riyadh as the capital. Al Masmak means 'strong and fortified building', as seen with its slits and bastions for defence.

The fort has a classic square design, with four round towers, one at each corner. There is a mosque inside the fort, which is now a museum dedicated to explaining the history of the Al Saud family. The upstairs levels are not accessible, but who needs that with so much information so well laid out in a multitude of rooms at ground level. Be sure to see the water wheel and well. The historic city walls were demolished in 1950. It is amazing to see pictures of Historic Riyadh as late as 1985, when demolition of the remains was (perhaps for today's tourists) sadly enacted. The walled mud city must have been an amazing sight, since the fort was only a tiny part of the whole area. North of the fort are a few lanes and alleys with old buildings that have survived the onslaught of modernity. This area is between the National Museum and the fort, if walking.

Al Masmak Fort

In 1862, the visitor William Palgrave recorded a number of facts about Riyadh at the time. The fort is located southeast of King Fahd Park in central Riyadh, just over three blocks along and almost due south of the National Museum / King Abdul Aziz historic centre.

Al Zal market has handicrafts, carpets and souvenirs and is close to the fort. It is open from 9am to noon and then after 4pm. Walking to the fort area took us 1hr, but no one really walks around this city – it's too vast.

> I have conquered this country first with God's grace then with Arab morality. My citizens are all soldiers; together we march as one. I never consider myself their superior.
> **King Abdul Aziz**

National Museum / King Abdul Aziz historic centre

This massive complex is set in a green park with palm trees, lawns and rockeries. It's a mix of ancient and modern Saudi styles, with many buildings, alleys and a vast entrance area with a coffee machine. Car enthusiasts can view the collection of royal vehicles set out in the King Abdul Aziz Memorial Hall. Out in the back area is the renovated Al Muraba (Al Murabba'a) Palace, a classic Arabian-styled structure. It was the private residence of King Abdul Aziz.

There are 8 main halls, covering topics such as the Early Man in the Universe, the Arab kingdoms, the pre-Islamic period, the hall of the Prophet's (pbuh) Mission, the hall of Islam and the Arabian Peninsula, the first and second Saudi State, the Unification of the Kingdom, and the hall of the Hajj and the two holy mosques – perhaps one of the most interesting exhibitions for those non-Muslims who cannot visit the actual places.

For those needing sustenance, the street behind (west side) has food options if the stay in the museum is a long one.

Bus 7 passes north of the complex but hardly any were seen. Taxi costs quoted to us were between SR25–35 for 5–10km, but it seems totally a question of luck, timings, traffic, plus bargaining.

Olaya Street

Olaya Street is the main road of the downtown area, with most of the high-rise modern skyscrapers; it's worth a stroll. The Faisaliyah Tower, with its golden ball set in a soaring spire, is one to see. Other structures include the Kingdom Tower, and several other dramatically designed structures aiming for the skies. The Faisaliyah Centre is about 5km from the Avenue Mall/Lulu supermarket, for example.

Modern souks

The modern idea of a souk is the covered, expansive and airconditioned malls – not quite as animated and colourful as a traditional souk, but definitely a 'sight' to check out. It's the goods on offer, the people and the cafés that will attract. People-watching is a pastime here for visitors and probably locals alike. There are at least twenty major malls around the city, with the central ones being Olaya, Al Faisaliyah, Moussa Centre, Hyatt and Royal Mall, along the downtown Olaya Street (currently disrupted by metro construction).

Saqr Aljazeera Museum
This unusual museum charts the history of aviation in the kingdom, with several aircraft on display. It's on the Eastern Ring Road.

Modern Riyadh, Olaya Street

Diriyah

Close to Riyadh on the northwest side are the ancient remains of Diriyah (locally called Addiriyah). The site is considered to be the birthplace of Saudi Arabia. It was attacked by the Ottomans in the 20th century but in recent years there has been a restoration programme. UNESCO is to list it as a World Heritage Site.

The site mirrors the history of the Saudi state, illustrating the rivalries of the past between the Al Saud and Al Wahhab. The mud brick structures are amazing and represent the 'royal' side of history. The Salwa palace is very impressive. The many mosques, both old and new, are another significant feature here. Wadi Hanifa runs below the site, with walkways on the east side offering views across to the mud structures through the shady palm trees.

Diriyah

Unfortunately gaining entry is even more complex than finding the historic settlement. Coming from the ring road, the route goes through the suburb of Diriyah and turns south at a fuel station. Turning right (west) the road drops a little to the Welcome Reception Centre on the right, with parking.

Diriyah is closed for renovations at present (March 2020). We were informed that it might be necessary to book online a day before the intended visit. Try at info@dgda.gov.sa for tickets – it's not obvious how this will work yet, as renovations are on-going and the site is closed to visitors. Entry cost is unknown at the time of publication.

A narrow road runs along the wadi in a generally southerly direction through the oasis (to the north is a no-photo zone). This way out is via some very narrow lanes, perhaps not recommended, but does eventually climb out to the plateau south of the ruins (no views although the high-rises of Riyadh are visible). A bigger road links easily from here to the Outer Ring Road for Makkah and Jeddah.

Close to Riyadh

Edge of the World
This impressive outcrop is northwest of Riyadh; it's a popular retreat at weekends. Called Jebel Fihrayn locally, it is part of the great escarpment of Jibal Tuwayq (also Jebel Tuwaiq) that curves around vast swathes of the desert. It lies outside Riyadh north of highway 505, and a 4X4 is required to reach it. Those without a 4X4 can take the main road towards Jeddah to see the impressive cliffs as the road descends.

Faisal's Finger
Locally called Kashm Zubaydah, this is a finger-shaped outcrop southwest of Riyadh just north of highway 80. It cannot be accessed without a 4X4.

Jebel Tuwayq west on the Riyadh – Jeddah highway

Other: Useful phone numbers in Riyadh: Police 999, Car Accident 993, Ambulance 997 and Fire 998.

105

Northern region

There's no simple way to arrange all the towns and sights to suit all journeys, so we have listed them in rough loops as the **Northern region** from Jeddah to the Jordanian border and back, plus the **Southern region** from Jeddah to the Yemeni border. The **Central region** and Al Jawf are listed later as other loops and additions.

Jeddah – Madinah (4–5hrs)   420km

Once clear of the Jeddah airport junctions, the route north is along the dry scrub of the coast to Thuwal. Be sure to fill up with fuel before Thuwal, as there are few thereafter, and many are closed. There are no designated laybys either.

The road (route 15 – also 45) heads inland and climbs imperceptibly through brown hills and along valleys. About halfway is **Al Asan**, with fuel and after that is the Sasco Palm services area, where buses stop. There are lava fields along the route, with distant low and high peaks, cone-shaped hills and jagged outcrops in view. The scenery becomes even more striking about 50km before Madinah. The city is surrounded by low but often vividly coloured rocky hills and ridges.

Foreigners must keep out of the **Haram** area, where the holiest mosque is located. See next paragraph for details. Be sure to always go left at junctions going clockwise and right for anti-clockwise here, to avoid inadvertently encroaching into the forbidden area.

Madinah (Medina)

Introduction

The second holiest centre of Islam, Madinah lies roughly 400km by road north of Jeddah. Non-Muslims are not permitted to enter the central area of the city. Currently the **Haram** area is delineated by the **Third Ring Road (King Khalid Road)** on the south and east of the city, and the **Prince Naif Bin Abdul Aziz Road** on the west and north, as the third ring road has not yet been completed around the whole of the city. **Many arched gates mark the Haram area.**

In 1974 we were able to take the ring road around the north of the smaller town, with a distant view of the great mosque and its green dome. It must have been what is now an inner ring road. Luckily we located a fuel station on this ring road, as supplies were horribly low!

Today there are still fuel stations on the ring road, but there is no chance of glimpsing the holy mosque, as construction in all directions has boomed.

Map of Madinah/Medina (not to scale)

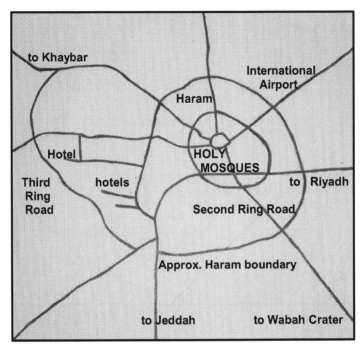

Please note this is only a sketch map, not to scale, and does not show all roads. It is merely an indication of the layout of the main roads and a few hotels around Madinah.

Getting there

The quickest option is to fly from Jeddah (or Riyadh). SAPTCO buses run a number of services daily. There appears to be a depot outside the Haram area on the left side of Prince Naif Bin Abdul Aziz Road, the main road to Khaybar. Check before travelling on this service about bus stops outside the **Haram** area.

The driving time in a private car is around 4–5hrs; probably less for a local! The road number is 15 and it's dual carriageway all the way from Jeddah and north to Khaybar. See road description above.

Accommodation

Non-Muslims will need to find something outside the city. Try Hotel Sobob (Sohab or Sahab) on Al Jameaat Road, SR150 for a good room. Food can be ordered in, but there is no café here. Next door is the green Hotel Diyar el Sidik, no sign in English, rooms SR150. Close to the roundabout is Al Badai, a little scruffy but OK at SR150.

A great new place is the Golden Address Hotel (from SR130) to the northwest, off the outer ring road in the Al Azizia district on Imam Muslim Street. Email; ok00200ok@gmail.com Tel 0566240121 & 0148691999. Groups might try this place.

Eating
Non-Muslims will need to find something outside the city. Al Baik is a popular fast food chicken and chips joint here and all over the country. Hotels can order food for delivery to the room.

Historical background
The origins of Madinah predate the coming of Islam, as it's a sizeable desert oasis. The earlier inhabitants of note were the Arab tribes of the Aws and Khazrai. A surprising fact about the history of Madinah is that there were also Jewish settlements in the oasis before the coming of Christianity. In ancient times it was called Yathrib and was a predominantly Jewish settlement. It is likely that the Jews moved here in substantial numbers after being expelled from the holy lands by the Roman Emperor Hadrian in 135AD. By 400AD the Jews had greatly aided the wealth of the oasis and were so influential as to convert the Yemeni Sabaean king Abu Karib As'ad to their faith. He in turn made it the state religion of Yemen instead of pagan faiths.

The Prophet Muhammad (pbuh) arrived in 622AD after his *hijrah* (departure) from Makkah. This date marks the beginning of the Muslim calendar. Madinah became the capital of the ever-expanding lands of Islam and is where the Prophet established the Muslim community (Ummah). Madinah was superseded as the capital in 661AD by the Umayyad caliphs, who made Damascus the new capital. In 683AD the city of Madinah was sacked by the Caliph, and the city lost power progressively to the sharifs of Makkah.

A volcanic eruption in 1256AD almost engulfed part of the city. Madinah remained a holy city despite various incursions. The Ottoman Turks arrived in 1517, but gradually they too saw a decline of their powers. In 1804 the Wahhabis took the city but were repulsed by a Turkish-Egyptian army in 1812. Between 1904 and 1908, the Ottoman Turks constructed the Hejaz railway to Madinah, hoping to control the pilgrim route for the Hajj. After WWI the Ottoman empire collapsed and the Sharif of Makkah gained some authority in the Hejaz until 1925, when the al Sauds took power.

The sights
For most tourists there are no sights, since all the historic and religious centres are off-limits to non-Muslims. The green-domed mosque in the centre of the Haram area is called the Masjid An-Nabawi. It is also known as the 'luminous city' (al Munawwarah) today. Madinah is also the place where the Prophet Muhammad (pbuh) was laid to rest. The first Caliph Abu Bakr and second Caliph Umar, as well as Fatima the daughter of the Prophet, were also laid

to rest here. The city once had a high wall around it – constructed during the 12th century AD with towers and four gates.

Gate marking the 'Start of Haram Area' of Madinah; non-Muslims must stay outside this zone

Sights **only accessible to Muslims** are the three sacred mosques. The first is the Masjid An-Nabawi, the main shrine. The Quba Mosque is another and the third is the mosque of the Two Qiblahs, which celebrates the change of the prayer direction from Jerusalem (the third holiest site of Islam) to Makkah. The Al-Rimah tomb of Hamza, the uncle of the Prophet, who was killed in the battle of Uhud in 625, is another holy site.

Despite the restrictions, the setting of the city is superb, with different suburbs separated by vividly coloured, small rocky hills and boulder outcrops. The deep blue sky, sunset colours and starry winter nights are calming, even if the traffic is not!

Richard Burton
Sir Richard Francis Burton was born in 1821 in Devon, England, and immersed himself in exploration and oriental study. One of his most daring adventures was to visit the holy sites of Islam. In 1853, disguised as an Afghan Pathan, he travelled via Cairo and Suez to Arabia. Having reached Medina (Madinah), he then proceeded to Mecca (Makkah), where he sketched the holy site. He published his memoirs describing the life of the people and the pilgrimages. He went on to the forbidden city of Harar in Ethiopia, despite the risks, and again published his discoveries in 'First Footsteps in East Africa in 1856'. He gained further fame following his exploits to discover the source of the Nile, and died in 1890. At least Burton did not have to deal with the traffic!

Mosque in the Madinah suburbs

Madinah – Khaybar (2hrs)   177km

The traffic in Madinah is as bad as anywhere, whether due to the volume of vehicles or the driving style. Tourists cannot drive into the inner area marked by arched signs, so keep well away and take a left if going around the west side clockwise and right if taking the ring road anti-clockwise. Route 15 (also marked 45) goes northwest out of Madinah. There is one SAPTCO bus depot on this route, which we believe will serve non-Muslim visitors. It is located at the junction of Prince Naif bin Abdul Aziz Road and Al Salam Road, just outside the Haram area.

Leaving the city, the route goes past palmeries much of the way, although most are well off the road. It's quite a scenic drive, with distant views to the east and west, and rugged peaks up to 1800m. One great massif with towering cliffs (possibly granite) to the east, is about 60km from the city. Dramatic foothills painted a dark striated brown and black are typical, with a splash of greenery – tamarisks, thorny bushes and some acacias.

About 15km before Khaybar is the significant settlement of **Al Thamad**. There is one new-looking hotel at the south end on the west side of the road, with an adjacent café. Another less posh is at the last fuel station on the east side going north. It's just at the turnoff to the white volcano, actually past the brown sign marked **Al Bayda**, also on the east side. If visibility is clear, the volcanoes can be made out to the east at some 50km distance.

Khaybar

Introduction

Khaybar has grown massively in the last 40 years since Bob visited. The new town is on the south and east side of the hills and quite extensive in area. The old oasis town of Khaybar is a picturesque place, with date palms and shady ambience. Old Khaybar is located where the brooding black lava hills and flows are cut by a dry riverbed (wadi) that only flows after unseasonal rains. This dramatic oasis is a veritable Garden of Eden that once had eight separate fortresses.

Getting there

The simplest way to reach Khaybar is by hired car, or travel agency car if money is of no concern. It's around 177km north of Madinah. There is no SAPTCO bus service listed at the bus depot in Jeddah but ask in case it's infrequent. Arranging the trip to Khaybar and into the volcanic area with a travel agent from Jeddah will be expensive, as most agencies only offer day trips to other places.

Getting into the **white volcano inner** area is only accessible by 4X4 or walking 10km each way, so visitors without a 4X4 need to hook up with the local people if possible. We did not find anywhere to set this up, so driving out to the volcanoes and walking is the better option for now. Local Bedouin drivers may help in providing a 4X4; see later under 'The White and Black Volcanoes' section for details.

Accommodation

There are a couple of places to stay in Khaybar, but as usual finding them is an issue. None are listed on the main booking websites. Coming back into town from Old Khaybar, just before the roundabout, on the right are two places, both unmarked. The better one is in the large Nadhi Pharmacy building and is called the El Farasi Hotel. It has large suite rooms that are OK but nothing great. It should cost about SR120, but we paid SR150 after hard bargaining. The other 'hotel' is to the right and about the same price. Google seems to think there is a better option further along on the right in a block back from the main street, but it was not found by us. Hopefully when groups start coming here there will be a better choice!

Eating

There is a good food shop on Route 15 before the old wadi turnoff going north. There are a number of 'restaurants', but they are all fast-food places and close by 6pm. Starvation again so back to bread and bananas – at least the supermarkets have a good selection of food, but they close at 6pm too. Beware! The fuel station where the buses stop is worth checking out during the daytime.

Historical background
The town was another significant settlement that serviced traders and later pilgrims on the route from the holy lands to Makkah and Yemen.

For a relatively insignificant settlement in 1974 and today, Khaybar has a surprisingly historic and important place in the history of the promulgation of Islam. The battle of Khaybar in 628AD between the Muslims and the Jews, who had been living in the oasis for centuries, was over possession of the forts. Jewish communities had also been living in Tayma and Madinah for almost a thousand years. According to historian William Montgomerie Watt, the Banu Nadir tribe might have linked with other Arab clans to fend off the onslaught from the Muslims of Madinah, who had already expelled the Jews from there. The remaining Jews had capitulated and agreed to give half their income to the Muslims, but later Caliph Umar expelled all the Jews. Many Jews later converted to Islam.

The three regions of the historic Khaybar oasis were al-Natat, al-Shiqq and al-Katiba, with each having fortresses on the basalt outcrops, above the palmeries and fields. The Banu Nadir and other clans of the Banu had already been exiled from Madinah in 625, but they besieged Madinah in 627 in the Battle of the Trench, also known as the Battle of the Ditch! The conflict was finally ended by the Treaty of Hudaybiyya in 628, when the forces of Islam ended their bitter feud with the Quraysh.

With a force of between 1400–1800, the Muslims set out for Khaybar in May 628. The forts of al-Natat and al-Shiqq fell early, but the stronger fort of al-Qamus was more heavily defended. Abu Bakr made the first advance and Umar made an assault later. The famous Jewish defender Marhab was finally killed in the assault under Ali in 628. The battle was decisive in the emergence of the new faith.

Khaybar's place in the history of Islam was made; afterwards it is little mentioned, other than for its position of the trade routes. It was also under the control of the Turks until 1915.

The sights
Close to the modern town to the northwest are the three separate ancient mud cities of Old Khaybar. Khaybar is the starting point for a visit to the White Volcanoes, the Harrat Khaybar lava fields and volcanic features to the east. The area hosts many astonishing geological features: multi-coloured cones, volcanoes and lava flows.

See more about the volcanoes under the Tayma–Madinah section, as it's perhaps better done on the return leg after Al Ula and the Wadi Qaraqir canyon via Tayma.

Old Khaybar

The road from the new town is off to the northwest diagonally from a roundabout on the northern end of town. Continue for around 2–3km. Look for a sign on the left marked 'Khaybar Cultural Village'. The track is rough but OK for just over 1km to the mud village. Sadd Qasr al-Bint is one of the largest ancient dams in the Kingdom.

Map of Khaybar (not to scale)

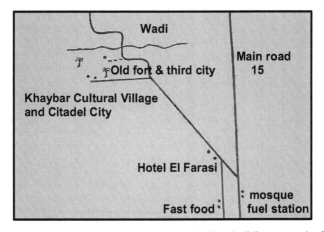

Some renovation is ongoing, but mostly the buildings are in fair shape here. Be sure to go to the northwest side of this **first city** of mud buildings, where the palmerie is seen below in the wadi. A few houses have original and quite striking doors made from palm wood. People were living in many of these houses in 1974.

Dominating this palmerie is the ancient **citadel city**, an amazing mud castle-like edifice with high walls and small windows, sitting on a sheer outcrop. The **third** separate **mud city** of Old Khaybar is further north along the sealed road. It can be accessed from a sidetrack to the left at a bend just before the road heads into the palmeries and wadi. This area is far more dilapidated than the first 'city', with a lot of crumbling mud houses. There are some interesting doors and a couple of places with green windows here as well.

In the central area is a restored mud mosque. Be sure to climb up the ridge to the south, where some tumbledown houses remain. The view to the north will reveal the ancient fort of Khaybar above the palmeries. It's a striking sight; enough to remind one of the old Arabia before oil was found. A new fence and staircase is being built to make this fort accessible – a sign of the future when tour groups may come. It's worth continuing along the track below the ridge to find a track on the right into the lush palmeries. The views of the fort reflected in the stagnant waters are exquisite.

Khaybar, Citadel village

Khaybar – Al Ula (3hrs+)   220km

Be sure to fill up with fuel, water and food before setting off, as it's a lonely road to Al Ula despite it being **the** place to see. There are a couple of large fuel stations in Khaybar where buses stop, one with a mini-supermarket and café; a tall mosque marks one good place on the Khaybar east side ring road.

Route 15 continues north for about 20km, where the turnoff west to Mada'in Salih and Al Ula is clearly signposted, 190km or so. This road is a single carriageway, so more concentration is required. Pretty soon the scenery is impressive, but the road is narrow and a bit rough on and off for 30–40km. Later the road has been widened and is great, with new, smooth tarmac. The scenery gets better and better, with brooding reddish and brown mountains and a few mini-oases of green. Watch out for the odd camel too. Banks of wind-blown sand are piled up the mountain slopes, with veins of white rock here and there.

About 80–85km before Al Ula the scenery is spectacular, and the road climbs up through a narrow **notch**. There is a lay-by around 175km from Khaybar (the only one to date between Jeddah to here via Madinah!).

Al Ula airport is about 25km before town on the north of the road near **Mogayra**, and already there are some striking rock towers and outcrops in view. The southern suburbs of Al Ula are 8–10km south of the main town. The oasis settlements of Al Ula are surrounded by palmeries, but there is quite a lot of housing as well. It takes 3hrs or so to drive from Khaybar to Al Ula at a modest speed.

Al Ula

Introduction

Expected to be the focus of most visitors' attentions, Al Ula is an amazing place surrounded by towers and canyons, enough to entice desert lovers, antiquity aficionados and everyone else as well. The town is located in Wadi Al Qura. The sights are enticing, the setting astonishing and the ambience memorable. It's also noted for the **Winter at Tantora** festival each winter between December and March, at weekends. North of Al Ula are the old city (Tantora), Dedan and Ekma. So far there is no obvious tourist information centre other than the temporary Winter at Tantora sales office in Al Ula North Park opposite the Royal Commission complex.

Al Ula is located on the easiest north–south route between the lava fields to the west and the steep canyons to the east. West of the town are the volcanic fields of Harrat Uwayrid. To the east are the sandstone outcrops of the Jibal Ath-Thumayid.

Getting there

The quickest option is to fly from Jeddah or Riyadh. A taxi from the airport to town is upwards of SR100; it is about 45km distance from the airport to the northern resorts in Al Ula. Buses run from Jeddah to Madinah, but there is no SAPTCO bus to Al Ula, so that's no use. There may be a service in future. The service listed by SAPTCO goes from Jeddah to Al Ula via Tabuk; it's also pretty dire. If already in Tabuk, no problem, as it's only 4hrs to Al Ula. The driving time in a private car from Jeddah to Madinah is around 4–5hrs; probably less if you are a local. From Madinah to Al Ula is around 5–6hrs. Take highway 15 from Jeddah via Madinah to Khaybar and then turn off on to route 375 north of Khaybar.

Getting around the Al Ula sights

Instead of the chaotic transport issues of Dec 2019, there are now three set bus routes for those visiting the main sights of the area (Feb 2020). Everything is much more organised, with a day ticket costing SR170 for any number of journeys. Buses run every 30mins during the Winter at Tantora period. This transport is required for entry. It is not permitted to drive to the attractions in your own car.

Red Line:	Winter Park, Hegra, Hujat, Nourah, Ekma & return
Thursdays	12.00 – 5pm
Fridays	8.30 – 6pm
Saturday	8.30 – 6pm

Blue Line:	Winter park, Wadi Alqura, Dedan, Ekma & return
Thursdays	12.00 – 9pm
Fridays	8.30 – 9pm
Saturday	8.30 – 9pm

Green Line: Winter Park, Shaden Resort, Sahary Resort, Elephant Rock and return to Winter Park.
Thursdays   Midnight – 12 Noon
Fridays   7.15 – 12 Noon
Saturday   7.15 – 12 Noon

After the end of the Winter at Tantora festival we were informed that tickets might be available at the entrances to some of the various sites, but it's not sure yet. It is not even sure if the sights will be open at all. Check: www.experiencealula.com or Twitter, Facebook, @WinterAtTantora and wat-customer-support@seera.sa

Accommodation

There are a few very expensive hotels, and these are aimed at visitors who can book them on the usual websites. The Emaar Tourism Resort located off the road to the south gate of Mada'in Salih costs SR750–1350, not including food or anything else. The Zahra Cottage Resort is well north of Al Athaib (Al Atheeb/Orteeb). In a side canyon before Al Ula there are two more upmarket places. There are other options on Booking.com, but all are expensive, some might say extortionate. Even these places don't offer food, not even breakfast it seems!

There are several local hotels in the town, but pre-booking is impossible thus far. On arrival try the following: Hotel Al Harbi, a smart red/white place on the west side of the main road through central Al Ula. It's not marked in English, but the manager speaks good English. Rooms from SR200–400. Two other local hotels are nearby, neither signed in English. One is down a side road to the east almost opposite the Al Harbi. There is a local restaurant (Derwas) opposite marked in English. The other, a less fresh place, is in the street a block south.

About 8km south of Al Ula there are three or four places near the Miqat hospital, on the west side of the main road. Another is near a fuel station south of the hospital on the west side off the main road. It's a bit overpriced at SR250, so bargaining may be in order. The Hotel Al Arac, once popular with expats, has been demolished and replaced by the offices of the Royal Commission of Al Ula, though not all locals seem to know that. Faisal Guest House, near the Dedan road and some impressive tower outcrops, seems a bit sleepy.

The cheapest good value place in February was the new Aistirahat-Al Sahab about 8km north of the Winter Park, on the left after Ekma. It's clean, has five rooms with fridge but no en-suite, shared hot showers and a communal kitchen, all set in a pleasant yard and garden. A room cost SR200. It's newly on Booking.com (GPS 26.725211, 37.88794).

Nasem Al Atheb tented camp is south of the road between Al Ula and Mada'in Salih and costs from SR350. There are Pakistani-made tents with carpets, power, kettle, outside toilet below and hot shower. (GPS 26.706309, 37.940471). Be sure to scramble up the outcrops behind the camp for great views at sunset and maybe sunrise; hiking boots are advised – be careful here. Further away some expensive resort camps are springing up., including Madakhil Resort, in a canyon a long way north of Al Ula, off the Tabuk road.

Eating
The town has a number of eateries for those not ensconced in the top-notch places. That said, very few hotels/apartments have restaurants, but food can be ordered from outside menus at hotel receptions. The Egyptian-run restaurant Derwas (Sherwas Corner Restaurant) down a side street near the Hotel Al Harbi has great dishes on display: beans, veggies, mince and pasta etc for good prices (SR13 for two dishes including bread). Heritage Garden and Sands of the Valley are a couple of other places we have not tested. Fast food is the norm in town and at the Winter Park.

Historical background
As one of the most verdant oases along the route from Damascus to Jeddah, Makkah and Yemen, Al Ula has always been an important stopover. Once camel caravans plied the route to Yemen, carrying frankincense to the holy places of the Middle East and Europe. There are some prehistoric carvings dating from the Bronze Age. Underground water was the reason for its development, allowing life to be sustained during dry periods.

The earliest civilisations in the region were of Dedan and the Lihyan. References to the Dedan civilisation found in Tayma suggest it dates back to the 7th century BC and gained its wealth and power from the frankincense trade. The Dedan empire was replaced by the Lihyan civilisation around the mid-5th to 4th centuries BC. The Lihyan empire ended with the rise of the Nabateans, who in turn were absorbed into the Roman Empire.

Much later, in 630AD the Prophet Muhammad (pbuh) led a campaign to confront the Byzantium Empire to the north. It is said that the Prophet spent 3 days in Al Ula. The oases to the south, including Mogayra, were more prominent in the past. In the 12th century AD the settlement of Al Ula became the main settlement, utilising some of the foundations of Dedan. It's characterised by stark red cliffs, strangely shaped outcrops contrasting with the bright green colours of the date palms.

Controlled by the Ottoman Turks from 1818 to 1915, the region was part of the Hejaz route. Charles Doughty, an English explorer, visited the Al Ula area in 1876, followed by the Frenchman, Charles Huber, who visited in 1883. German explorer Julius Euting accompanied Huber. There are no records of any fees or entry tickets they paid in those times! Today it is expected to become a booming tourist destination.

Map of the Al Ula area (not to scale)

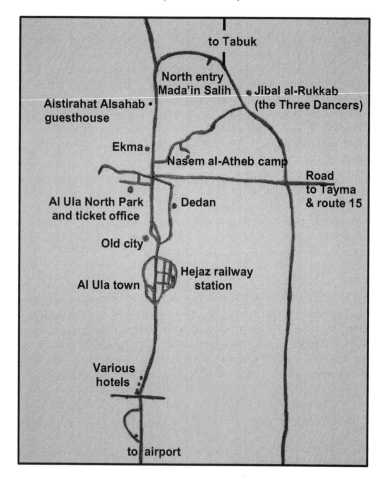

Note:

All these designated Heritage Sites are now said to be closed for renovations until October 2020. Check online in case they are opened earlier.

www.experiencealula.com

The sights

Musa Ibn Nusayr Fort
The remains of the ancient fort, Musa Ibn Nusayr, stand in Al Ula Heritage Village (Deira) and can be visited after a short, easy climb up steps. It has a great view of the old mud village and the oasis. It's just west of the main road and can easily be seen above the crumbling mud buildings of Deira, of which it is an integral part.

Deira
Deira (Ad Deerah) is a traditional mud village, which was founded 800 years ago. It was inhabited until the 20th century. Because of floods in the rainy season, it was built above the valley. It had over 1000 houses adjoining each other, forming a defensive wall around the village. Most houses had at least two levels, with the lower space being cooler. The old souk area is on the west side below the cliffs. The last people left the old city in 1983 and the mosque closed in 1985. The ticket office is on the south side but may be closed for renovation until Oct 2020. During the Winter at Tantora festival. tickets cost SR55 for the fort and old city.

Museum
The Antiquities and Heritage Museum is located in the main downtown area on King Fahd street. It houses items on the history and culture of the area, including Mada'in Salih and the Nabateans. Some information on the flora and fauna of the area is also found.

Dedan
Close to Al Ula (on the northeast side) beyond the old city are the cliffs on the east side of the canyon that host the remains of Dedan and the Lihyan civilisations. There are two areas; the first by the north gate was closed for renovations in 2019. Apparently this area has a fortified palace with four towers dating from the 1st millennium BC.

The southern site is open. The relatively small tomb entrances are seen on a shelf along the cliff walls near the base area. There are a number of separate tombs complexes. The most notable tomb has two lions above the entrance doorway. These animals represent strength. The remains of the Dedan civilisation at ground level are open. Various walls, cisterns and stone walls are located here. One ancient statue from Dedan is in the Louvre in Paris.

Entry costs SR55; you have to travel there in their bus/vehicle, despite it being only a short distance on a good road. During the Winter at Tantora festival, tickets were obtained from the main Al Ula North Park ticket office but it is probably closed now until Oct 2020.

Remains of Dedan, snake carving

Lion images at Dedan

Ekma

The rock art of Ekma (mountain heritage area) is north of the town and just north of the Royal Commission complex. The rock images are set into a substantial cliff running adjacent to the road to Mada'in Salih, on the west side of the valley. Entry costs SR55. With a lot of confusion about where to purchase tickets, we sadly missed this place.

Elephant Rock (Jebel al-Fil)

Much photographed and visited, the outcrop has an archway feature reminiscent of many found across the Sahara in Algeria, Niger and Chad. It is located about 7mins drive along route 70 that goes towards the main Tayma–Khaybar motorway. A sandy track goes to the north; it is driveable in a small car with care. It seems that tickets are available at the site, but do check with the information desk at the park, as it's already different from before. Entry cost SR35 + transport for those without wheels – that may mean the SR170 daily bus ticket. Otherwise walk around the outside fencing for views. Some locals and a European 4X4 were camping close to the site. Nearby to the west is the Siamese Twin Rocks outcrop.

Elephant Rock

Viewpoints

The main viewpoint on the cliffs west of town is accessed along a 17km tarmac road from the Winter Park/Royal Commission complex area to the west. It has some steep hairpins to negotiate, but any car will do it. The ride takes 30mins to the viewing area carpark, with several walkways; late afternoon is the best time for photographs as the sun goes down, but not too late as the shadows creep up the slopes quickly. The views over Dedan and, if early enough, the fort/mud city are very good; the whole panorama stretches from Mada'in Salih to the south of Al Ula.

The plateau up here consists of flat rocky lava. Other viewpoints are really wherever it looks safe to scramble up!

Ottoman Railway
Built between 1901 and 1908, it linked Damascus with Madinah. There were stations in Mada'in Salih and Al Ula. The Al Ula station is to the east of the old city, where a few buildings remain.

Farm visits & desert art
These are available from the Winter Park office in season. The desert art means a modern art display around 12km to the north, we understand, in a canyon. Entry is free and a bus might run from 10am to 4pm, but this needs to be checked with the park information desk.

Other places
Listed by the Winter Park information desk are Al Aqqura, Naqsh Zuhayr and Qurh (Al Mabiyot), all apparently north of town and probably rock art sites. Ask at the information desk.

Magic Mushroom Rock – North of Jibal al-Rukkab
For those with wheels, this trip gives a good overview of the Jibal al-Rukkab from a different perspective, without the cost and hassle of arranging a 4x4 trip. First head to the entrance of Mada'in Salih then take the road north to Breakh and **Tabuk**. This passes close to the escarpment, where it should be possible to walk in for around 1km and climb up on sand on the right of the cliffs. Further on the road climbs through a **narrow defile**, with views down into the canyons on the left. About 20km north of Mada'in Salih, take the road east towards **Al Jaharah** (113km). Initially it crosses a more open plain; there is one particularly striking outcrop to the north, with stripy patterns and a single tower. The views to the south illustrate the tangled maze of Jibal al-Rukkab and there are 4x4 driveable tracks into the area. About 30km from the last junction is an **amazing 'Magic Mushroom'** rock on the right. This is as far as we drove east.

The 'Magic mushroom' rock

We learnt that, going another 15km east, one should reach **Garamil**, where some free-standing outcrops can be seen (images of these appeared in the 'Directions KSA' January 2020 magazine).

Just north of the turnoff is another Hejaz railway station called **Abu Taqah**. Still further on north and then west is the much-photographed **Madakhil arch** which requires a 4X4 to visit. On the return drive there is a coffee shop on the left 3km before the narrow defile.

East of Al Ula – South of Jibal al-Rukkab
It's worth going a few kms east of Al Ula from Winter Park on the road that passes Elephant Rock. Continue east past the main junction; this road joins the Tayma–Khaybar road eventually, but there is no need to go very far east other than for curiosity. There are some super views of the southern outcrops of Jibal al-Rukkab, as well as looking west towards the Al Ula valley.

Jibal al-Rukkab
The exceptionally enticing area of Jibal al-Rukkab is northeast of Mada'in Salih. This whole area is dissected by sand-filled canyons with sheer walls running generally east-west and north-south, although others break the pattern. The main outcrops of interest are nicknamed the Three Dancers (al-Ragassan), being three towers close together.

Al Ragassan (The Three Dancers)

Side trip: Jibal al-Rukkab – Al Ragassan 4X4   (3–4hrs)
This is a fabulous side trip from Al Ula and should not be missed by desert aficionados. It is not cheap, though, with prices from SR1200 for car and driver. If business is slack off-season, it might be less at SR1000. It was not easy for us to organise the trip below, and on our first visit in December 2019 it was not possible. Even on our second

visit, it took two days and three options before it all fell into place; this may have been because all the vehicles were busy at the weekend.

The route begins near Al Hafar in the agricultural area east of Mada'in Salih. The route leaves the tarmac and skirts around the last green circle before heading into a wide sandy canyon/wadi with high, sheer-sided cliffs. A few palm trees cling to the northern cliff edge, with many stunted Sahel-like bushes. This first stage is very sandy and soft with quite steep drop-offs early on; driving is definitely only for those with dune experience. Tyre pressures need to be lowered before this stage.

The wide area continues and, after a side chasm, the route turns more to the south. After a few minutes it comes to a gaggle of amazing towers on the left;

one is quite jagged in shape. The sandy route does a series of smaller turns again with steep sand banks, sparse vegetation, incredible canyon walls and haunting chasms like slot canyons. Multi-shaped turrets and towers dominate the terrain in all directions en route.

It is about **10km** and takes 20–25mins to reach the famed **Al Ragassan** outcrops, 'The Three Dancers.' Set below the high cliffs and standing in golden sand, the dancers are given a great backdrop. Two smaller outcrops sit on the south side watching the spectacle. Walk around and peer through the gaps that separate the closely entwined threesome.

View south from among the dancers

For a different perspective, it's possible to climb to the south, where three **quirky outcrops** sit half buried in the deep sand

dune bank. It's a wild spot with amazing views, including the dancers. Al Ragassan is a great spot for lunch and a drink.

Towers near Al Ragassan

To avoid returning the same way, some trips continue east along the wild canyon into more sandy areas overshadowed by sheer walls. This route twists along in deep sand to two more isolated **dancer-like outcrops** near two **side canyons** that hide their own secrets. Ahead the next canyon narrows and there is a very dark, slot-style defile on the right. Soon follows a '**fallen tower**' leaning against the canyon wall. It seems as if there is no way out from here, but around the next corner the route passes between low **mud-like walls**. It takes only 10mins or so to reach here at speed from Al Ragassan.

Panoramic view at Al Ragassan

Dominated by sheer walls that threaten to block out the sunlight, the way passes two slot canyons on the left and snakes around to cross a **wider canyon** running north–south. After a few more narrow ravines through lower cliffs, the route bursts out into more open country. The cliffs are left behind, and the outcrops are lower and more rounded. Very quickly the **open** **desert** takes hold, with outcrops further apart. In less than 10mins there is a dry circle on the right and shortly a large **green crop circle** on the left. The route is on a vague piste now and is much faster. A strange **knobbly outcrop** appears to the left (west). The more distant outcrops still hold interest on both sides of this wide wadi valley.

Mud canyons, sand and cliffs

In Jibal al-Rukkab

All too soon the piste hits the northern road mentioned above under the **Magic Mushroom** **Rock** trip. It's around 20km from the Three Dancers to the main road, so not a day walk!

Thanks to our skilled driver Faleh for the adrenalin rushes, and to Mohammad Al-Anazi for organising it.

Thanks also to Bander: Bander@arabneurs.com (The Explorers)

Trekking options

This vast area has great potential for some exploration and for extended trekking itineraries of a few days. Backed up with 4X4 support, any number of camping-based treks can be entertained.

Madakhil Arch

This option can be combined with the Al Ragassan trip and makes a great finale to a fabulous desert adventure. Coming from the Jibal al-Rukkab Three Dancers piste, the route heads west along the road to the **junction** with the Mada'in Salih – Tabuk road. Heading north towards Tabuk, first is the railway station of **Abu Taqah** and then about 9km further on the right is a small diamond-shaped hole in a strange humpy outcrop. Quite soon the route to the arch leaves the highway for the gravel road to a farm near the **Madakhil Resort** and then heads off among the sandy outcrops.

Madakhil Arch

A **three-fingered** outcrop can be seen to the north, topping a higher dark wall of rugged continuous fractured outcrops. Ahead is a more pointed hill topped by a **castle** wall-like summit.

The fabled **Madakhil Arch** is found in a wide plain surrounded by outcrops and distant ridgelines. It's an amazing structure not dissimilar to some found in Utah at the Arches National Park. It must be a great prospect to camp beneath the arch on a typical starry desert night. Truly a night in a hotel of a thousand (million) stars.

Mada'in Salih

Introduction

Perhaps the most famous historic sight in Saudi Arabia after the holy places and Jeddah, Mada'in Salih (Maidan Saleh) is fabulous. It was the first UNESCO World Heritage Site in the country in 2008. The ancient city was sustained by underground water (using tunnels and wells called Qanats) and thus was a site where humans could flourish. It means 'cities of Salih'; Salih was a Thamudic prophet who lived long before the coming of Islam. Around 25km north of Al Ula, Mada'in Salih is in Madinah Province.

The original builders of the city were the Nabateans, who called the city Hijra. The Romans called it Hegra. It is known locally as Al-Hijr and it was the 2nd largest Nabatean city after their capital, Petra in Jordan. The Nabateans, who were traders of frankincense, occupied a kingdom that stretched from Damascus in the north to Mada'in Salih in the south. They also extended their domains from Sinai in the west to Dumat al-Jandal, the capital of Al Jawf in the east, roughly along the border with Jordan. They traded with places as far away as Kos in Greece, Cyprus and Rome. Unlike Petra, where only one inscription allows dating, the Hegra sites have many such defining plaques. In 106AD the conqueror Emperor Trajan integrated the region with Rome as a province in Arabia until end of the 3rd century.

Getting there

To be honest, we have no way of knowing what access will be permitted in future, but it is expected to open to the public in October 2020. Once inside the site fencing, a 4X4 or bus operates around all the places of interest. In Feb 2020 transport by bus was used by all from the **Winter at Tantora** festival headquarters – Al Ula Winter Park, marked on Google Maps but not Maps.me. Tickets were being sold at the information desk / ticket office in Al Ula North Park. Entry to the site is from the north (the main entry point at present) adjacent to the Ottoman Hejaz railway station.

By private car it's 25km and 30mins drive around the spectacular northwest loop to the north gate entrance and another 25mins continuing around clockwise and back via Athaib (Atheb or Otheeb) to Al Ula town. Taxis may be available in future, but turning up at the site entrance hoping to buy a ticket will probably not work, as it **did not** in Dec 2019 or Feb 2020. See our sketch map below.

Getting in

In Dec 2019 the entrance ticket cost SR75 plus SR119 for the return bus transfer per person from the Al Ula Winter Park. In Feb 2020 it was SR85 and the all-day hop on – hop off bus cost was SR170. Visitors who followed us all reported not being allowed to drive to the entry areas of the sights and this was still so in Feb 2020. The south gate was not in operation. Visitors were given a pre-programmed plastic card on a lanyard to enter. The online pre-booking system was very hard to navigate, if not impossible, for the first weekends of the Dec 2019 – March 2020 season.

It's not yet clear what will happen in future; keep checking online forums and blogs. See www.experiencealula.com, the official website, though it has no information about future access at the time of writing this book.

Accommodation
The hotels are all in Al Ula at the moment, see above.

Eating
Currently there are no food or drink facilities at Mada'in Salih, so take water and snacks.

Historical background
The area was first inhabited from the 3rd millennium BC, when the Thamud tribes came to this location rich in underground water. It was they who gave the area its name Mada'in (meaning cities) Salih, in honour of their prophet Salih.

Salih
The name Salih comes from the historic prophet known as Salih. He was a preacher during the Thamudic period, long before the coming of Islam. The most famous reference to Salih is linked to the story of the she-camel of god that was a gift to the Thamudic people when they acknowledged that he was a true prophet. Salih is also mentioned in the Quran and the books of the Bahai faith.

Jebel Ithlib

The Thamudic civilisation

The Thamudic civilisation existed in the Hejaz region from the 8th century BC until close to the period that Islam arose. The oldest known reference to the civilisation comes from an Assyrian inscription dating to the reign of King Sargon II in 715BC. Prior to this civilisation were the Ad, who inhabited the Hadramawt in southern Yemen and may have been part of the same clans. The Thamudic people may have originated from Southern Arabia and moved close to Mada'in Salih. Evidence for this are some rock inscriptions on Mount Athlab nearby. The Thamudic script is similar to the Semitic. The Quran mentions the Thamud in the Surah Al A'raf, warning about the judgement time to come. The scholar Ibn Khaldun refers to the Thamudic civilisation in his works Kitabu I-ibar (Book of Lessons) of the 14th century. In the context of the history of Mada'in Salih before the Nabateans, the term Thamud may have referred to the civilisation of the people who moved there from Yemen and Southern Arabia. It has been suggested that the civilisation was wiped out by a volcanic eruption.

Later the Dedanites and Lihyanites settled in the area in the 6th to 4th centuries BC. Dedan was a powerful civilisation in the region, with its capital in modern-day Al Ula. It had its own language and became wealthy from the caravan route that passed through the canyons. The Lihyanites were the part of the same civilisation, but they ruled later. The domains extended south to Yathrib (modern area of Madinah) and as far north as parts of the Levant. They held sway around the Gulf of Aqaba, which was then called the Gulf of Lihyan. The people are considered by Arab scholars to have belonged to the Ishmaelites and perhaps from Abraham.

Their civilisation was succeeded by the Nabateans, who came in the 1st century BC, making Hegra their second settlement. They moved south after the Romans threatened their main capital of Petra. Utilising the skills learnt in Petra, they began the massive works at Mada'in Salih. However, in 106AD the Romans finally reached this second centre and integrated it into their empire.

In all there are thought to be 111–132 tombs, depending on the classification system. The site first developed in the 1st century AD and is still not fully excavated. There are seven main areas, together with the Jebel Ithlib group. The southern area was used by the military. The whole area may have been some sort of military zone set up to secure the trade routes. It was inhabited until at least the 4th century and maybe as late as the 6th century AD. Then it was abandoned, and the people moved to Al Ula, but it retained its significance on the trade routes.

The Necropolis

The Necropolis (defined as the area of the enclosed antiquities) contains 111 major tombs; 94 have decorated facades. The facades tell us a lot about the social status of the incumbent, their wealth, the masons, the religion and the military ranks, if any. The smallest is 2.7m and largest is 21.5m high. The sculptor cut from the top, working downwards. The tombs at Petra date from 50BC, but these were cut around the time of Christ. Mesopotamian influence is evident in the design. Other features are linked to Egyptian, Assyrian, Greek and much later even to Roman influences.

The most important tombs were reserved for the elites, their bodies wrapped with fabrics impregnated with resin. There were also over 2000 tombs for other people, just dug into the ground or on the rock. Some tombs have Nabatean texts above them, generally giving details of the deceased within. The inscriptions on the tombs date from the 1st century BC to around 75AD. Extraordinarily, one tomb dates to 267AD, a long time later. The tombs vary in size from tomb N3 at Jebel al-Mahjar to the largest at Qasr al-Farid (tomb N110).

Features on the tombs

The tombs have many designs, with eight different styles notable at Mada'in Salih. Common are the simple burial sites; others include those with **merlons** (a five-stepped triangle) on the facades, like the lion tomb (N92). Some have a single row of merlons, others two rows and there are also **half-merlon** styled tomb facades. The tombs with the proto-Hegra 1 style are the most commonly seen, with a variation that is classified as the proto-Hegra 2 group. An example is the tomb N42 of the Qasr al-Bint group. The Hegra-style tombs are the most intricate and can be seen at Qasr al-Bint and Qasr al-Farid (N110). It is thought that the **eagle** carvings seen in numbers are the vehicles that enable the souls of the deceased to fly between each other.

The tomb outcrops are listed in alphabetical order, but on the ground, this may not match a tour around. Most tours begin with Jebel Ithlib and then go to Qasr al-Bint, Jebel al-Ahmar and end at the lone Qasr al-Farid.

Jebel Ithlib

The Nabatean holy mountain of the area, east of the al-Bint group, it is surrounded by some dramatically sculpted outcrops. Cutting through it is the **sacred siq**, a smaller version of the famed one at Petra. At the entrance to the siq is the diwan, a rock-cut assembly area. It is believed that Dushara, one of the Nabatean deities, worshipped here. The niches along the siq contain statues of the deities. The siq leads to the temple area, where religious ceremonies took place. A water channel and cistern were built here to facilitate the ceremonies. Visitors are not permitted to go past the siq area. Greek and Nabatean inscriptions are also found on site along with steles and altars.

The siq entrance of Jebel Ithlib

Raised tombs of Qasr al-Bint: double row of merlons on the left, and two half merlons on the right

Jebel al-Mahjar (A)

Jebel al-Mahjar, meaning quarry mountain, is north of the Hegra centre and has 14 tombs (1–14) carved into three outcrops. Tomb N3 has the smallest façade (3m) of any in the whole site. One of the outcrops has evidence of being a sacred place at its summit. One tomb of note here is N9, called the Taymanite's Tomb (ie from Tayma). It has 53 burial niches and two inscriptions. The tomb was carved in the 13th year of the reign of King Aretas IV. It was constructed for Hawshab ibn Nafi and his two sons, who were indeed from the oasis of Tayma.

The eastern outcrop has three tombs (N12, 13 and 14). Tomb 12 is for Shubayt ibn Aliyu and is the only one with a Nabatean script. Shubayt was a Jew, and his wife together with their children are noted in the inscription. The tomb was carved in the 3rd year of the reign of King Malichus II around 43AD; it is important for illustrating the fact that the Nabateans embraced other races.

Outcrops near Jebel Ithlib

Qasr al-Bint (B)

Northeast of Hegra centre, it is named after the daughter (bint) of the founder. This group contains 31 tombs (N17 to N46), most carved from the same outcrop, with some of the most impressive sights and a lot of Nabatean inscriptions. Tomb N24 was commissioned by Abd'Obodat ibn Aribos and his daughter.

Qasr al-Bint: N44, Doctor's Tomb

Be sure to see the impressive tomb N44 – the Doctor's Tomb (below) with its triangular-topped façade. Another tomb not to miss is the Lion tomb N37 as well as N39, the oldest tomb of Hegra. The unfinished tomb N46 would have been the largest in Hegra if it had been completed. It demonstrates how the Nabateans carved downwards from top to bottom in construction of the facades. The tomb sits above tomb N17 with only a little carved out.

Qasr al-Bint: Amazing relief at the Doctor's Tomb, showing snakes and flowers

Qasr al-Bint: N39, the oldest tomb (double merlons)

Qasr al-Bint: N37, the Lion Tomb

Jebel al-Ahmar (C)

Known as the Red Mountain, Jebel al-Ahmar has 19 tombs (N112 to 130). One story about the Tomb of Hinat's daughter Wabhu arose when in 2011 bad smells aroused interest. This led to the discovery of 80 body bones and a woman's remains wearing a neckless made of dates, said to be for the deceased to eat in the next world.

Jebel al-Ahmar: tombs 112 & 113, built in Proto Hegra I style

Jebel Al-Ahmar: Hegra style

The north side of the Jebel Al-Ahmar group has some very well carved and more complex designs. One of the best is seen above.

Flower motifs and a classic double line of merlons are clear to observe on the next page. The right-hand façade has a much simpler design; perhaps a less wealthy client was entombed here?

136

Jebel Al-Ahmar: Flower decorations and double merlons

Qasr al-Farid (D)

Located in a large area, there are three tombs here (N109 to N111). It is N110 that attracts a lot of attention, since it the largest structure of Hegra. Often known as the 'lonely palace', this chamber was built in an outcrop used exclusively for this tomb. It was made for Bani Lahin ibn Quza but failed to be completed. The facade has a crown of two half merlons with Egyptian-style cornices resting on 4 Nabatean capitals.

The 'lonely' tomb of Qasr al-Farid

Jebel Khraymat (E and F)

The Jebel Khraymat contains 53 tombs (N48-101). Set to the west there are 53 tombs (N48 to 101). Tomb 64 is the Centurion's Tomb; it has been damaged by flash floods, as have some others in the area. The tomb was carved by Aftah for Sa'dallah ibn Zabda (the centurion). Close by is tomb N66, which is called the Prefect's Tomb. It was made for Matiyu the son of Euphronius - the prefect, and dates around 40AD. The most impressive and largest of the group is tomb N100. The statue above the doorway has kept its head, with four columns above. This tomb has the Hegra-style design. It dates from 64AD and was carved during the reign of King Malichus II for the family of Tarsu ibn Taym. The arched tomb of Jebel Khraymat (N92) is unique and located here.

Unfortunately, this area is not always open to visitors; apparently some restoration work is ongoing.

As-Saneh Tombs (G)

At the southern end there are seven tombs (N102–N108) of which one is large – Qasr al-Saneh (N102). It dates to the reign of King Aretas IV Philopatris. This area may not be open to visitors.

Diwan / Triclinium

Called diwan in Arabic, the triclinium were carved out recesses with seats on three sides. They were used for musical performances and the like. At least six such structures have been found around Mada'in Salih, with the most noted at Jebel Ithlib. Some Nabatean scripts are found near the diwan area, again indicating the owners of the sites. As well as the Nabatean scripts, there are a few that belong to the Thamudic period and the much later Islamic era. In addition, a few Greek and Roman texts are found here.

Over 130 wells, cisterns and drainage systems have been discovered across the area, designed to save rainwater and collect it for human sustenance.

Ottoman Railway Station

Part of the defunct Hejaz railway, it was constructed in 1900 by the Ottoman Turks to link Damascus with Madinah to facilitate a quicker passage for the pilgrims during the Hajj. It was originally proposed that the line would continue to the holy city Makkah. However, T. E. Lawrence (of Arabia) and his allies blew up the line during WWI. With the demise of the Ottoman Empire, the line fell into disuse.

Today the stations and a fortress here have been converted as museums to house the old locomotives. It's at the north entrance to Mada'in Salih, with a locomotive and a few carriages as well as various sheds.

Hejaz railway station at Mada'in Salih

Final memories of Al Ula

Little remains of the old civil generations of Medain Salih, the caravan city. The clay-built streets are again the blown dust of the wilderness. Their story is written for us only in the crabbed scrawlings upon many a wild crag of this sinister neighbourhood and in the engraved titles of their funeral monuments, now solitary rocks, which the fearful passenger admires in these desolate mountains.
Arabia Deserta, **Charles M Doughty 1888**

No longer sinister, Al Ula will surely become a star attraction in Saudi Arabia for tourists of all persuasions – the curious, those captivated by history and archaeology, and those who seek to explore on foot.

Al Ula – Wadi Qaraqir West (4–5hrs)   **300km**

Perhaps one of the best drives in Saudi Arabia, this route offers sensational scenery, the equal of any of the more famed destinations across the world. Be sure to keep the fuel tank topped up on this lonely journey. Timings allow for some photo stops.

From Al Ula the route is first south to the airport junction near Al Mogayra. Taking route 8776 right, the road is mostly good heading west through brooding brown hills with ridges and rounded outcrops of little distinction. It takes about an hour to **Al Balata**, where there is fuel. The road is also marked to Al Wajh on the Red Sea coast and would be an alternative approach from Jeddah via Yanbu to avoid Madinah. The next stage is to the junction for route 8451, just before **Bada** (also with fuel). The scenery is again hills of multi-coloured shades of brown.

About 170km from Al Ula, the route makes a very dramatic steep climb up the escarpment and on to a plateau area (50kms wide). The road cuts through a zone of pinkish strange-shaped outcrops known as the **Al Magaza** (mountains) to the junction for Al Shwaq (Ashwaq), which is about 32km from the escarpment top. A sign indicates it is 47km to Shwaq from here and after 18km a sensational view opens.

A great ridge line of turreted and towering features decorates the **red cliffs** that appear ahead, high above the brown hills and sandy plain below. The road is incredibly steep down (low gear). The skyline is dominated by the fabulous red jagged cliffs for the descent. Americans might think it's a bit like Monument Valley and Bryce canyon rolled into one.

Shwaq is a developing town with new buildings on the west side and fuel stations. There appears to be a basic hotel above a fuel station area. There must be something better, but we didn't find anything obvious. If a suitable hotel can be found, this is the place to stop before the Wadi Qaraqir canyon.

Be sure to turn right near a few planted palm trees and a brand-new road for **Disah** in the dune area out of Shwaq (not signed in English but a brown one in Arabic). It's around 40km to Disah across the low dune plain.

There are no obvious hotels in Disah (Dissah), although there might be one up a side canyon north of town, where streetlights and a communication tower can be seen in the distance. It seems unlikely, though, for now.

The whole canyon of Disah and ahead into the wadi is stunning, with red cliffs, amazing outcrops, vivid green palm trees – a veritable paradise. It is 11km to the end of the road from Disah. The whole side trip is 70km from the main road junction to the end of the wadi.

Road to Wadi Qaraqir

Amazing outcrops near Wadi Qaraqir

Wadi Qaraqir (west)

The 15km-long canyon has road access from each end. It is a 'must see' sight if time allows. At the western end, the cliffs soar to 300m high, while at the eastern end of the wadi, they are over 100m. A small stream runs through the canyon on the western side. Palm trees paint the canyon vivid green, in contrast to the stark reddish-brown canyon walls. Here and there bright green, grassy areas spring to life adjacent to the water, when it breaks the surface.

Side trip: Wadi Qaraqir Walk (3–4hrs)   6km

It is possible for 4X4 vehicles to get into the sandy canyon, but it's really much better to go on foot. Avoid Fridays and Saturdays if you want the canyon more to yourself. Although it's is possible to walk right through the canyon to the eastern side, it's a long trek and would need additional transport at the other end. For most visitors, just hiking in a few hundred metres is enough to capture the atmosphere. We walked about 3km into the canyon, which easily gives a great overview of this fantastic paradise. Timings are approximate, since taking pictures here will delay progress.

From the roadhead, the main sandy track continues along the stream bed and, if walking, water flooding could stop progress. Another sandy track is to the left (north), which goes through palm trees more easily to the stunning slender outcrop that is the hallmark of the canyon. Actually the tower is massive and it takes 20–25mins to get to its western base from the end of the road.

The canyon floor is quite wide now, with a number of streams and pools that will depend on when it last rained. About 15mins from the tower base it was necessary to keep to the right to avoid thick reeds and wet ground after a sandy bank. It may well be necessary to walk through the streams in the canyon floor. The canyon bends around to the right a little, with a fabulous grove of deep green palms to the left. This leads into dense palms, but is eventually a dead-end side canyon with some amazing outcrops towering above. A shady area offers a good lunch spot if needed.

The main canyon now bends to the right, with sheer cliffs ahead. Tall reeds are found along here, backed as always by the fantastic fairytale turrets and towers of the red-walled canyon. Soon the route turns to the left and heads into more dense vegetation. Continuing on, the canyon walls are less high, but the outcrops are still impressive. The main canyon continues through a narrow gorge between the lower cliffs. Just to get this far, with many stream crossings, took us 1½hrs. The return walk is slightly quicker, as the ideal route is known. We walked for 3hrs, but obviously continuing further is possible. The main snag with this whole area is the lack of accommodation; carrying sufficient camping equipment and food is a major logistical issue.

There is still no obvious place to stay in Disah, although the side road to the north between Disah and Wadi Qaraqir has a couple of places at the end that might eventually become possibilities. No one was around when we visited in February 2020. Hopefully some accommodation options will develop here. In February we drove back to Duba (1½hrs), mainly to explore the Red Sea coast route via Al Wajh to Al Ula. The route via Shwaq is much more exciting.

Wadi Qaraqir trekking

Wadi Qaraqir at sunset

The eastern entrance to Wadi Qaraqir canyon is 80km south of Tabuk on route 8900 and then west on route 8788. The walk into the canyon is much longer from this roadhead, but generally wider.

Wadi Qaraqir – Shigry (2hrs)   140km
Making a total of around 6–7hrs drive from Al Ula, Shigry is a good stopover for the night, saving the 'battle' in Tabuk at rush hour.

From the Disah turnoff, the road heads west for 45km to join the main **Duba–Tabuk** motorway. The northbound carriageway of the motorway is the old road and it's a rough ride for a while until the new section is reached.

There are massive, rugged mountains to the west.

The motorway climbs up an amazing new stage to reach another plateau area and runs on across the flat plain to Shigry.

Shigry

Shigry is surrounded by low outcrops, with the Al Shaq canyon to the northwest of town – jeeps are required for a trip here. There is a fuel station on the main road, with a supermarket that stocks camping gas cookers. The complex hosts a daytime café and night-time takeaway. There are a few large but basic rooms for SR120. Apparently, a couple more hotels are to be found here in Shigry.

Al Shaq Canyon

Apart from isolated outcrops, the main sight is the great canyon of Al Shaq. It is the so-called 'Grand Canyon' of Saudi Arabia. The canyon walls are over 300m in height and the views are from the rim. The nearest settlement is Shigry, around 4km from the main Duba–Tabuk motorway (route 80). There are also Bronze Age structures in the vicinity, dated to the 3rd century BC. Currently access to the canyon is possible only by those with a 4X4 and good walking boots.

Shigry – Tabuk (1hr)   80km

It's an easy drive on a good road, with great scenery all around.

From Shigry the low, wind-carved outcrops are exchanged for rolling plains and low hills dotted with what looks like semi-nomadic plots. In fact, the area has a number of so-called Bedouin camps for visitors, but access requires 4X4. One place is called Mdhal Camp, but it's not marked in English as yet.

This area has some outcrops of note and reddish sand and is about 40km from Shigry.

Traditional Bedouin tent

Tabuk province

Close to the Jordanian border and similar in geography, this area is sure to develop quickly. There are fabulous canyons, not unlike those of Wadi Rum (in Jordan). The **Sarawat** mountains on the Saudi side of the Red Sea rise to around 2500m. The volcanic but dormant features of the Harrat Al-Uwayrid are part of an upland area located 120km east of the Red Sea. Bedouin legends recall eruptions around 640AD that killed their livestock.

Road to Tabuk from Jordan, 1974

If visitors are permitted to cross into Saudi Arabia from Jordan in the future, the northern part of this region will benefit from any boom in tourism. For now, the most sought-after sights are around Al Ula and Khaybar, in Madinah province. The main and only sealed road in 1974 was via Tabuk, Tayma and Khaybar to Madinah. Many roads exist across the area today.

Historical background
The northern province is noted for the discovery of some of the oldest human remains in the country near Tayma. Tabuk was on the trade routes from Yemen to the Middle East even in Roman times, two thousand years ago.

The province is also on the route from the great cities of the Middle East – Damascus, Istanbul and Amman – to the holy city of Makkah/Mecca. Pilgrims have travelled this way since the 7th century and merchants even longer, trading goods like frankincense from the Hadramawt in Yemen to the Levant and Europe for vast profits.

146

Along the Gulf of Aqaba and inland are the ancient heartlands of the Nabatean kingdom that lasted from the 1st century BC until 106AD. Very little recorded history followed, until the region became part of the Muslim empire 10 years after the birth of the religion.

In the 16th century the Ottoman Turks controlled the region. They ruled over the lands from around 1516 until 1918, when the colonials arrived. With Constantinople as their capital, they held sway over vast areas of the Balkans and the Middle East, as well as the Hejaz of Saudi Arabia. Their empire crumbled with the end of World War I.

The Hejaz railway was built by the Ottomans in the early part of the 20th century. The province was retaken by King Abdul-Aziz Bin al-Saud in 1926.

Tabuk

Introduction
It's over 45 years since Bob drove around the tiny settlement of Tabuk in 1974. The regional capital Tabuk, once a sleepy backwater, is the main transportation hub. Modern Tabuk has grown into a major city, with over a million inhabitants. Located on the pilgrimage trail from Damascus to Makkah, the town has always been a crossroads of trade and commerce. The town is not without its own attractions for a few hours. The Hejaz railway ran through Tabuk and the old railway station, now a museum, is a sight worth seeing. However, driving into a big city like Tabuk is demanding, so consider if it is worth the hassle for only a couple of sights.

Getting there
The simplest way to reach Tabuk is by plane; it's a long way from Jeddah or Riyadh. SAPTCO run a bus service from Jeddah along the coast, taking 14hrs, departing at intervals throughout most days. Times may vary each day, so check before travel. There are also buses from Riyadh. Mr Abu Salih has been recommended for those wishing to hire a 4X4 with driver, tel: 053 3365 774. Prices from SR400 per day.

Accommodation
As usual, check the major booking websites, which are more up-to-date than any guidebook.

For a cheaper option check out the Al Eairy chain of furnished apartments. There are at least six on offer around Tabuk. A good one is on the north side near the massive Lulu hypermarket. It's called Al Eairy 2 and is on Booking.com from around SR85 upwards for a simple but comfortable room with bathroom.

Eating

We do not have any recommendations. There was nothing obvious in 1974! But it's a real city now and has loads of options for fast food. The Lulu supermarket has enough for days of cheap eating; hummus, labneh, foul medames, fresh fruit, pastries, tinned fish etc.

Driving around Tabuk, a modern roundabout

History

Being close to the great civilisations of the Middle East, Tabuk has a rich tapestry of archaeological remains. The history of Tabuk probably dates back to the time of Ptolemy, who refers to a place called Tabuka or Tabawa. Pre-Islamic poets refer only to a mountain called Hasmi in the area. Tabuk was also the scene of a battle in 630AD, as the Muslims expanded their domains. The European explorers Doughty and Huber visited in the late nineteenth century.

The sights

Tabuk Castle

Locally the castle is called As-hab-al-Aykah; it is mentioned in the Quran. It sits on the site of a castle that may be traced back to 3500BC. The Turkish hero Sultan Suleiman the Magnificent had it rebuilt in 967 and another Turk, Sultan Mehmet IV, worked on it in 1064. The last restoration was in 1652. The site later became the location for a Turkish fort. The forts and castles, including this one, along the pilgrimage route gave security to travellers en route to Madinah.

The current structure has two levels, a courtyard and a mosque. Finding this place near the city, having to negotiate such a large sprawling town, is daunting. The stone square structure sits within a fenced area, but was closed during our brief visit here. Park in the blocked-off street to its immediate north.

The Prophet's Mosque

Once an ancient mud mosque supported by wood similar to some in Mali, this mosque was known as the Repentance Mosque. Some scholars believe this mosque is one of the oldest in the world, dating back to 630AD, when the Muslim forces reached the area. It was restored in 1632 and again during the reign of King Faisal. We never did find it.

Tabuk Museum

Located in the old Hejaz railway station, it was renovated and opened in 2019. The building is a blend of early 20th century and contemporary architecture. Different rooms detail the city's and the country's long history from pre-Islam to the future. It also houses traditional Saudi artefacts. One room is dedicated to the achievements of the founding of the kingdom in 1932. The Ottoman period is also detailed. Another room is dedicated to the Nabatean civilisation, with a huge wall illustration of the tombs at Mugha'ir Shu'ayb (also known as Al Bada or Al Bact).

There are a number of station buildings, sheds and railway paraphernalia on the south side, where some parking offers the chance of a few photographs through the fencing if the site is closed.

Tabuk old Hejaz station and museum

Tabuk – Northern Canyons Loop

The northern route between Tabuk and the Gulf of Aqaba is home to some amazing canyons and outcrops, just waiting for trekkers and visitors. Similar in appearance and geologically linked to Wadi Rum region in Jordan, this area is thus far hardly known.

Tabuk – Al Bada (3–4hrs)   252km

It's an absolutely enthralling drive through fabulous scenery. Those with a 4X4 can escape into the desert canyons and outcrops of Jebel Hisma and Wadi Dham to the south. Those with normal vehicles can explore closer to the road. There are outcrops surrounded by sand and later an amazing canyon with sheer cliffs soaring from the red sand dunes. Be sure to keep the fuel topped up. Timings for the drive vary, with so many possibilities for photo stops.

The road from Tabuk to **Bir Ibn Hirmas** is quiet, with farms and some circular crop areas. There's little to detain anyone in Bir, except refuelling for the longer stretch to Al Bada. After open country the road passes into rocky stretches and eventually into fabulous scenery of sand banks and amazing sandstone outcrops. This area is the northern part of the **Jibal Hisma**. The **Wadi Dham** area of Jibal Hisma is to the south from here, and can only be reached by 4X4 and a guide.

Close to the Jordanian border in 1974, we saw great outcrops and canyons, similar to those further north at Wadi Rum in Jordan. There is tremendous potential here for desert trekking (and more modern pursuits). As yet it's hard to get any information about the possibilities, so watch this space. The pictures included here and in the introductory section illustrate the typical scenery in 1974. Little has changed, except that there are now more people in the valleys.

Jibal Hisma

Similar in appearance and features, Jibal Hisma is related to the wadis and canyons of Wadi Rum. The outcrops are part of the same range of uplands, which stretch for around 200km from Wadi Rum to the southern limits. It is located between Jebel al-Lawz in the west and Tabuk in the east. Jibal means a collection of rocky formations, which may cover hundreds of kilometres.

Wadi Dham

Wadi Dham is probably the most spectacular wadi of the Jibal Hisma area. It is 20km long, with rugged hills. The Wadi Dham area hosts a treasure trove of rock art and inscriptions that date from the Palaeolithic to the Islamic period. Human and animal figures can be traced to the Thamudic, Greek and Nabatean periods. Some rock art found here has Kufic Arabic inscriptions dating back to the early years of Islam. A 4X4 is required to access the wadi.

Desert west of Tabuk in 1974

Side trip: Jibal Hisma North Walk   (1hr)

For anyone who relishes desert scenery, this area is amazing. There are towering sandstone outcrops of all shapes and sizes, mixed in with sand dunes and sandy slopes. To appreciate this area, it's best to walk. Just over 100km from Tabuk there is a layby parking area on the right and soon a communications tower. Then approximately 1km west on the right is a **vast sand bank** reaching up to some jagged cliffs and towers. We parked at 28.866572°N, 35.885768°E.

Unfortunately there is no parking here other than the side of the road or the central reservation. In retrospect it might be better to park in the layby and walk up the road, or try the track nearby off to the right. When we came back from our walk there were two bemused policemen in a car next to ours, wondering if we had broken down or got lost perhaps!

In the event they were extremely helpful and no questions were asked in any language. Probably parking on the roadside is an issue and, to be honest, it's not a great idea. It really would be better to stop in the layby before our start point, follow the dirt track off to the right and find a way to our area with GPS.

As for the walking, it's amazing wherever is chosen. We climbed up on the east side of the sand bank, quite steeply to a rocky viewpoint. The views, even from here are superb, looking across to the south towards the flat-topped plateaux of **Jibal Hisma**. In the foreground there are small canyons and shattered, eroded red cliffs. Dropping down the tiny sandy gully, we made off north across the hollow and climbed through a gap in the rocks to the northwest. There is an amazing wall of cliffs with turrets and towers ahead with a massive rock balanced on the ridge. A few hardy plants survive here.

To the east through the darker outcrops appears to be the track that leaves the road after the layby.

Jibal Hisma, a trekking paradise

Continuing up to the next sandy ridgeline, the views are totally amazing; reminiscent of the Tassili Plateau in Algeria. Looking south across the **Jibal Hisma plateau**, the panoramic view is even better. From the top of this sandy ridge it's just a short walk to the edge of a small cliff with wild scenes to the north.

This is about as far as it's worth walking. A nomad tent could just be made out in the distance.

Warning

Although we did not incur any issues walking here, it is as well to remember that this is a **border area** and we do not know if such activities are appreciated. In addition there are Bedouin tents around the cliff bases in places, and we do not know if they all approve of tourists walking around their canyons. A local told us, "if it's not fenced off, it's OK." Ideally ask at a check post if possible! The whole area along this road is surely number one for potential treks; a couple of days with local guides and full camping gear would be ideal.

Back on the road now, further along west for the next 20km, there are a number of places that look good for a short stroll to observe the fabulous rock formations. The cliffs are different here and higher, with more rounded features. There are sandy areas backed by high cliffs with some strange-shaped ridges. Hidden chasms with dry springs and eerie canyons add to the atmosphere.

The next 20km is also sensational, as the canyon narrows and the cliffs get ever higher. There are some amazing erosional features decorating some of the towers, like razor-edged crenelations. The road descends soon after the last of the red sand-filled canyons to the junction of the main road north to Haql and the Jordanian border, and south to Al Bada.

(A small road heads south to the Jebel al-Lawz area but we did not take this, as it is said to be a restricted area near the mountain.)

Jebel al-Lawz

The highest peak in Tabuk Province, south of the main Jordan–Tabuk road (394), is Jebel al-Lawz (2549m). Its name means Almond Mountain. It's actually a mountain in shape, as opposed to being merely a high upland; snow can top its summit in winter. The area has some ancient rock art sites featuring cows. It can be accessed by small road, but it is not permitted to get too close as it lies in a restricted zone.

The route to Al Bada from the junction at **Al Sharaf** is also a scenic drive, with the high peaks of Jebel al-Lawz and the Sarawat to the east rising in a crescendo of ever higher jagged ridges. There are dry wadis and isolated farmsteads most of the way to Al Bada.

Al Bada

Al Bada, also called Mugha'ir Shu'ayb (cave of Jethro), is a little-known Nabatean site. It is generally thought that the remains of Al Bada are the ancient city of Madyan. Thus far 33 tombs have been found in the area of Jebel Mussalla. The area was visited by Burton and Philby, among others.

Al Bada is a small spread-out town with a sleepy atmosphere that is appealing after the frenetic traffic of Tabuk and thus not at all bad! Located in Wadi al-Abyadh (also called Afal in the lower reaches), it lies a short distance northwest off the road (route 55) and due south of Aqaba. This road continues towards the Red Sea, heading south to Ras ash Shaykh Hamayd.

Map of the Gulf of Aqaba

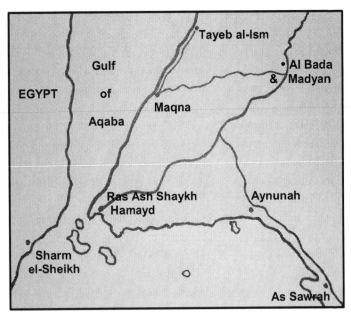

There are a couple of apartment places in the first part of town, but finding anyone to deal with the administration could be an issue. About 10km south is another part of Al Bada where Booking.com offers an apartment for around SR150. It's simple but comfortable with bedding provided and a man was on hand to assist. There is a sign next to the door: AMAN phone 0559192563. Before this, however, is Madyan.

Madyan (Mugha'ir Shu'ayb)

The ancient Nabatean remains of Madyan are not on the scale of Mada'in Salih, but there is a peaceful ambience to the site, with magnificent views of the **Jebel Ash Shifa**, part of the Sarawat mountains.

The complex is on the west side of the road and, despite on-going excavations and renovations, entry for us was free. Walkways led in from the entrance building slightly uphill to a series of white pathways. The first sight on the left is up steps, where three hollows are found in the outcrop. The last one to the left is accessible, with empty vertical tombs inside. The other two openings are smaller. The next four small tombs are quite impressive, with the left tomb having good detail. The next has a flower-like carving on the left. The third from the left is empty and the one on the right has some merlons above the doorway.

View of Madyan (Mugha'ir Shu'ayb)

Ancient Madyan

Madyan is believed to be the place where Moses found refuge after escaping from Egypt. It is generally accepted that he met the prophet Shu'ayb here. The prophet considered Moses a compassionate soul and gave him his daughter in marriage. He stayed here for 10 years with his new family before returning to Egypt to set his people free of the Pharaoh, Ramses II. The biblical parting of the waters of the Red Sea is legendary and scholars believe that Moses and his people came to Wadi Tayeb al-Ism. References to the people of Midian appear in the Bible and the Quran.

Continuing along the path, there is a small archway on the left and around the corner are three more tombs. These are notable for the vertical tombs inside. The pathway descends and climbs to the most impressive **two tombs** up in the hillside of Jebel Mussalla. The left-hand tomb is less well decorated but inside is worth a look. The right-hand tomb has some clear merlons and inside are empty tombs. Just adjacent on the right appears to be an eroded tomb with little inside but a good view looking out. Finally, to the west and very high up on the hillside, is another arched, hollowed out area with tombs. The approach is rocky and scrambly and, since there is no path, it's not clear if one should go there.

Opening hours are 10am–6pm daily except on Friday and Saturday, when it is 4pm–6pm only.

Tombs at Madyan

The Gulf of Aqaba & Red Sea

When Bob inadvertently reached the coast some 80km south of the Jordanian/Saudi border in 1974, it was completely deserted. Unable to read any Arabic, they took a wrong turning and stumbled on it by accident, with their transit visas nowhere near long enough for further exploration. The azure blue calm sea looked inviting. To be sure this coast will see more concentrated development. The towns of Sharma, Al Muwaylih and Duba in the north, plus Al Wajh and Yanbu (a modern port) much further south, will probably be sites for expansion. This whole area is destined to become the Sharm el Sheikh of Saudi Arabia, with the development of the **Neom** vacation complex and luxury hotels.

Al Bada – Maqna (30mins)   35km

It's a short drive down through dry hills to the Red Sea, and then a spectacular drive north along the coast.

Head back to the central/northern area of Al Bada and, at the roundabout with dolphins/fish in the middle, go west (it's not marked to Maqna in English). The road descends gently through barren brown hills with some greenery to the north. Suddenly, from a crest, Maqna and the Gulf of Aqaba are seen below. Egypt and the stark outlines of Mount Sinai are almost due west across the biblical waters.

Maqna and the Wells of Moses (Al Bir Sa'idani)

At the start of the town, before descending into the centre, look left to see a dirt road leading to what looks like a well surrounded by palm trees. Just after this are a few buildings, one of which is said to be a hotel, and a mosque. This is the top of the 'Wells of Moses'. In fact they are the twelve springs that relate to the twelve tribes whom Moses led from the Sinai. Maqna was also the site where the Muslims engaged the people of Judham, who later converted to Islam. Apparently there is an archaeological site near the wells that relates to the birth of Islam.

With views across the Gulf of Aqaba toward the resort town of Dahab and the mountains that surround St Catherine's Monastery on Mount Sinai, the Wells of Moses are more significant for the history attached to them rather than for any dramatic sight.

Moses in the Land of Midian

Moses is said to have spent ten years in the region here and Al Bada after his escape from Egypt. Then this area was known as the land of Midian. Traditional legends say that Moses came from Egypt to Maqna and to the wells of Sa'idani, where he helped two girls who were collecting water. The girls' father (Shu'ayb) realised that Moses was a compassionate man and gave him one of his daughters in marriage. After Moses brought his people out of Egypt, they lived happily in Midian for many years.

There is parking by the wooden structure, from where a pathway leads down through palm trees to a small bridge. Already the first springs are visible. Continuing down under the low palm leaves, there are lush green reeds and the sound of rushing water hidden beneath. Further down the springs are to the right, while even lower down the palms thin out and to be honest there is little need to go further. The wadi below is heavily used for agriculture and many buildings look private. It is possible to try to approach the springs from the coastal end, but it's all very developed in the wadi.

The wells (springs) of Moses

Maqna – Tayeb al-Ism (20mins)   25km

From Maqna roundabout the road heads north, passing a complex on the left. It runs along the coast, passing small bays and a few beach areas with some shelters. The road undulates along with great views of the **Red Sea**, the rugged mountains to the east and, after rain, the green vegetation in the wadis. Ahead the cliffs rise dramatically, nearly sheer from the sea. The defile of Tayeb al-Ism can be made out as the road passes a check post before following the narrow terrace above the waves to reach Tayeb al-Ism (also Tayeb al Esm).

Wadi Tayeb al-Ism

Known as the 'Canyon of Moses', this incredibly narrow defile is virtually hidden. The mostly dry channel runs into the Red Sea with the mountains of Sinai across the Gulf. Towering, sheer and overhanging cliffs dominate the chasm. Palm trees offer shade at the entrance to the canyon. A gate blocks the coastal road further, and during our visit a police car was stationed here.

Side trip: Tayeb al-Ism walk (2–3hrs+)   10km

Access is possible by vehicle but only for 200m, where rocks block any further progress. This perhaps is a blessing, as the walk through the defile is amazing and tranquil. Take snacks and water; even in winter it's a long trip to the so-called **Seventy Palms** just beyond the cliffs to the east. This defile is said to be the route Moses took when he arrived from Sinai.

The first stage is through the incredibly narrow defile, with perhaps the highest cliffs of all in the chasm. The valley floor is stony and initially flat, with a barely perceptible rise.

People at the entrance to the Tayeb al-Ism canyon

The views soaring above are enough to give anyone neck ache. In 10mins the driveable section ends, then it's another 5mins to the first palm tree. The chasm bed becomes wetter, as various small streams flow for intermittent sections. There are a few bends, with looming cliffs above. Some large **boulders** have fallen on to the chasm floor.

Around 45mins from the start, the defile widens out with more vegetation. Evidence of **flash floods** can be seen, with the few trees (some tamarisks) collecting debris around their trunks. The gradient increases and around the next corner the ravine narrows. Around another corner palm trees threaten to block the way, but not quite. The route continues to yet another corner, and ahead the palms and greenery increase significantly, with more streams underfoot. Close to the streams are a dusting of **salt deposits**.

The blackish colouring of the water seems to be from the algae-like residues on the stream beds. As rain threatened, we stopped after this, just before a bigger loop in the canyon. Look at Google Earth before your visit!

Apparently it's about another 2km to the Seventy Palms from here. We understand that apart from the many palms and luxuriant vegetation, there is little else to see. It took us 1½hrs slowly to reach here, and 45mins back downhill.

Tayeb al-Ism canyon walk

Maqna – Duba (2–3hrs)   190km

Instead of retracing the route to Al Bada (unless staying two nights), take the coast road south. It's a deserted route along the dramatic shoreline.

Less than 8km along here is the diving resort, Hotel **Hasco**. It's a pretty posh place and charges SR400 in winter and SR700–750 in high season (April–May).

The public areas are filled with fascinating diving memorabilia and the Egyptian manager is a mine of information. Continuing south the road remains empty, passing the blue waters of the Red Sea on one side, and on the other, striking cliffs and later red sandy plains with mountain views as a backdrop. Further south, the mountains are lost to sight and the flat plain is slightly surreal. Eventually this narrow road comes to the main highway.

Going right for 6km or so is **Ras Ash Shaykh Hamayd**, noted for its sunsets, but we turned left for

Duba (and Al Bada.) The dual carriageway continues around the large bay to Al Kiri, Ay'nunah and the 'resort' of Al Sharma, with expensive and not so great hotels. The Sarawat mountains are particularly jagged along this stretch to Al Muwaylih, where the fort is not obvious and not signposted.

It's a fast run down the coast to Duba, passing the port and ferry dock for Safaga in Egypt.

Duba

Duba is a pleasant town with a great harbour area full of small boats. Overlooking the harbour is a large square fortress, with towers and a massive doorway. Inside there are various rooms around the courtyard, but little else so far.

There are also some old houses and buildings dotted about his area, and some renovated walls and towers. It is possible to drive along the Corniche from the fort to regain the main road, north to Tabuk or south to Al Wajh.

Duba harbour

Just after entering the town, at the first roundabout there are two hotels and some shops, plus a fuel station on the road going left (route 50) for Tabuk, Shigry and Wadi Qaraqir. Hotel Al Blagha has good rooms for SR205. The other hotel is the Tal Al Sahel, which is less expensive. Across the road is a Herfy fast food outlet for burger fans (SR21–26).

Duba – Wadi Qaraqir (1½hrs)   135km

Following route 50, the road climbs from the coast into dark rugged foothills with views of the Sarawat Mountains – Jebel Shar and the more distant Jebel Dibbagh, all the northeast.

The road is not initially a dual carriageway and work is ongoing to finish this section of the main route to Tabuk from the port of Duba. About 40km on, the junction for Disah is on the right. This is a country road but quite fast, leading into ever more scenic mountains and sandy plains. About 55–60km along here, watch out for the left turn to Disah; it's only signed in Arabic but is near a line of newly planted palm trees soon after a small settlement.

The road to Disah crosses a sandy plain and eventually climbs into the Wadi Qaraqir area. For hiking in the Wadi Qaraqir Canyon, see page 142 for details.

The paradise canyon of Wadi Qaraqir

Tabuk – Tayma (3hrs)   **260km**

The description now continues on the main northern loop. It's a relaxing drive on a good road once the city has been left behind!

Tabuk is a large modern town with very new housing blocks and a clean appearance. It is about 25km around on the south side ring road. From town the road is dual motorway with a few rough zones. The countryside is flat with low brown hills, but not far from town there are a few quite high sand dunes to awaken the interest. Mostly it's a fast but featureless trip until the junction of the road to Al Jawf, near the Sasco fuel station on the east side carriageway. This road continues east to Iraq and Kuwait. The junction is 108km from Tabuk ring road exit. Tayma is around 145km south.

Continuing south, the plains are broken to the west by low black lava fields some way off. About 30km before Tayma are the low but scenic outcrops to the east of Medealah 'mountain', as the brown sign indicates. There is a fuel station nearby.

Tayma

The oasis of Tayma is perhaps the oldest inhabited settlement in Saudi Arabia. A bone found here might be as much as 90,000 years old. It's always been noted for its water sources and wells that were so sustaining in the days of camel caravans along the pilgrim route. A recent inscription find has been traced to the Egyptian Pharaoh, Ramses III. Surrounded by the sandy desert of Nefud al-Kebir, it's located on the sight of a former lake long gone since desertification has taken hold. It's a pleasant town, without the frenetic traffic of Tabuk or Madinah.

Getting there
Tayma is a long way from Jeddah (830km) or Riyadh (1045km). The drive from Tabuk is noted above.

Accommodation
As usual, check the major booking websites, which are normally more up-to-date than any guidebook. The well-appointed Jewel Places (not signed in English on the outside) is on the south side of the main road into town; it is on Google Maps and booking.com. Discounted rooms are from SR225, but most cost more at SR300. As usual there is no restaurant or food on site.

Eating
There was nothing obvious in 1974, but it's a real town now! There are a number of chicken-and-chips, KFC-type places around town. The Turkish restaurant was closed for holidays. North of the Jewel Place Hotel, across the main road northwards, are a gaggle of fast-food eateries/takeaways. No sign of any hummus or foul beans.

There must be better options, but after a 360km drive, energy to find them was lacking. Be sure to keep a good stock of fruit and food from the supermarkets for this journey, as it's remote.

Historical background

Tayma paid tribute to the Assyrian king, Tilglath Pileser III in the 8th century. It was also recorded in a Mesopotamia-Babylonian text implying that it was one of six oases conquered around 552BC across the northwest of Saudi Arabia. Nabonidus was the last king of Babylon; he is thought to have built the settlement wall in the 6th century and lived briefly in Tayma. A stela was found here in the 19th century and it is now in the Louvre museum in Paris. Another stele with Aramaic inscriptions, linked to those of Axum in northern Ethiopia perhaps, is also in the museum. A cube-shaped stone is another strange curiosity on display, linked to worship of the sun and moon.

The Spanish explorer Benjamin de Tuleda visited the oasis in 1170, claiming a Jewish prince was the governor; a fact not substantiated. In 1181 the French crusader, Renaud de Chatillon, attacked a Muslim caravan near Tayma, breaking the truce between Saladin and King Baldwin IV of Jerusalem. Charles Doughty came in 1877 for mapping purposes, and soon afterwards in 1883 Frenchman Charles Huber arrived to claim the stela.

Map of Tayma (not to scale)

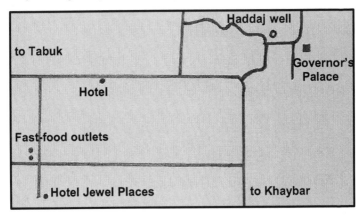

The sights

Haddaj Well

This is located in the old city area of Tayma, east of the new town. Set in a circular enclosure, the well sits centrally with wooden drawing wheels. This structure is believed to have been constructed in the 6th century by Nabonidus. It is said that 99 camels were used to draw water here. It was not open, but one can see through the fencing sufficiently to get an impression. Entry fee unknown.

Governor's Palace and old city
Nearby are the remains of the mud-brick palace/fort used by the governor of Tayma. It's a picturesque building that has been partially renovated at the front, west side. Currently still being improved, the east side has impressive mud walls. Various towers are part of the high main walls. There is a small mosque next to the palace, which may be open in the morning. Inside there are many rooms and a courtyard area that is still under renovation. Close to the wells and the Governor's Palace are a number of derelict mud buildings, including a small mosque. There is an alley near the palmeries that gives some idea of what once must have been here.

Al Hamra Palace
Located roughly northwest of the wells are the remains of Al Hamra. It's best accessed around a ring road adjacent to the extensive palmeries away from the built-up areas; follow your nose or smartphone down the various streets, first going west and then north from the wells. The stone remains probably date to the 6th century BC and again are linked to Nabonidus. This site was also closed for renovations, so we have no idea of the entry fee or what can be seen.

Governor's Palace, Tayma

Tayma museum
Tayma museum is one of the best in the region. It details the Neolithic, Bronze Age and Babylonian periods in the area.

Harrat Uwayrid

The lava fields near Tayma were explored by Charles Montagu Doughty between 1876–78. Getting near them is an issue.

Nefud al-Kebir

Northeast of Tayma is the extensive desert of the Nefud al-Kebir. Meaning 'great sand dune desert', it stretches 290km between Tayma and Ha'il in the east and is up to 225km wide. It is connected to the Dahna, the narrow arc of dunes that almost encloses all of the western region of the country, stretching over 1300km from north to south and bending around in a huge curve in the east to join the Rub al-Khali in the south.

Al Naslaa

The Al Naslaa outcrop consists of a single rock split vertically down the middle. Theories suggest that this is a natural phenomenon where one side of the rock balances on two supports dropped slightly. It is located close to Tayma, although we did not visit it. Ask locally to find transport to it.

Camping south of Tayma 1974

Tayma – Khaybar (3hrs)   256km

It's an exciting drive through more volcanic and sandy scenery. There are virtually no fuel stations on this stretch and it's a wild ride. The old city of Khaybar can be explored after the drive.

After Tayma the main highway crosses bleak open desert for a while, before some distant outcrops and a higher isolated massif to the east.

Closer to Khaybar the road snakes into the dark lava fields and the hilly volcanic features of the **Harrat Khaybar**. There is an old road running close to the motorway to the west, which is a more scenic option after the Al Ula turnoff. However, it's a bit rough for a small hired car, so it's better to stick with the main highway.

Just before Khaybar is the turnoff west to the old mud settlements of 'historic' Khaybar. This road heads northwest to the wadi and palmeries of the old city and fort.

It's a lonely drive to Khaybar

White and Black Volcanoes

The **White Volcano** area is sure to attract keen explorers and those interested in geology. Some volcanoes are painted with cream-coloured pumice-like flows that contrast with the dark flows of Jebel Qidr. The white volcanoes are basically cones covered by a layer of light-coloured material that burst upwards from the ancient interior.

Covering 14,000 sq. km. the area hosts a 100km-long series of vents, volcanoes, scoria cones, lava domes, basaltic lava flows and the layered strato-volcanic feature of **Jebel Qidr** (2005m). The region only recently stopped being active in geological terms – some 1500 years ago. This involved the flows from Jebel Qidr, with its brittle, glass-like lava fields.

Jebel Bayda (1913m), the largest crater, and **Jebel Abiadh** (2093m) are the two main volcanic features topped with this white, silica-rich material. Both names mean White Mountain in Arabic; Bayda is the feminine form of the word and is an almost perfect circular tuff ring with a wide flat crater inside, while Abiadh (Abyad), the masculine form, is a higher lava dome with a summit crater.

Jebel al-Aqir (1865m), a hat-shaped peak, is another startling feature of the area. The whole area is characterised by the mixing of the different outflows: white, such as from Jebel Bayda, and dark from Jebel Qidr. Look out for a few camels that delight in the rich scrubby plants that cling to life in the dormant craters that litter the area.

Scoria cones on the side of Jebel Qidr

Geology of the volcanoes

In the deserts of Saudi Arabia, the geology comes right to the surface and in full view, as there is no soil or surface cover to hide it. These vast lava fields and flows are called **harrats**. They are, in the main, flows from **shield volcanoes**, which have very fluid lava that runs easily for large distances when molten. These basaltic flows are often quite thin and leave whirlpool-like features in places. Such features can be seen on the walk into the volcano complex. The eruptions of material continue for long extended periods, thus giving rise to the large areas of the flows, such as the Harrat Khaybar. Other types of volcanic eruptions flow from **cinder cones**, **strato-volcanoes** and **lava domes**; these are much more viscous and cool quickly to produce steeper-sided, classic cones.

The white and black volcano area is amazing, since almost all types of volcanic activity are represented in one area. The highest cone, Jebal Abiadh, is a lava dome, while the white Jebel Bayda is a tuffic ring with a shallow crater hosting a cinder cone. The white colouring of the Al Bayda and Al Abiadh cones is made of pumice-like, comenditic ash, that includes areas of silica-rich, obsidian and other pyroclastic materials. Amazingly the obsidian appears to have been mined in Neolithic times. These two white volcanoes are related more closely to the crustal cones of the East African Rift Valley system, and not to the harrats that surround them.

The black cone of Jebal Qidr is a strato-volcano of the Hawaiite class that erupted in historic times with flows of dark lava. The flows are of a glassy nature in places. There are a couple of amazing vents on the northern side of the volcano.

Getting there

The good sealed road goes northeast from Al Thamad 15km south of Khaybar. Al Thamad has two possible hotels, as mentioned earlier. En route are a few isolated houses of Al Rahba village, with many speed bumps. Once on the open road, the volcanoes on the horizon begin to get more impressive. The road crosses Wadi Al Jool, where a sign about 40km from Al Hamad marks the sidetrack to Um Jarsan Cave. The many cones of the main volcano area are directly ahead, with different flows and small, deep, eerie gullies of the lava seen on the way. En route there are also a few jagged lava tongues where the flows have finally solidified.

The road climbs gradually to around 1700m, to a sign marked Harat al Rass al Abiad to the right. On Google Earth this track seems to be one access route along a sandy wadi to the west side of the white volcanoes. The main road climbs to a high point and slightly down to the buildings and Bedouin settlement on the north side of the area. It's about 75km from Al Thamad. Park at 25.75002°N, 39.97316°E.

From the roadhead park (we'll call it Bedouin Camp, as the settlement is not far east), it will probably be necessary to take a Bedouin jeep (if available) to get much closer without walking. Jebel Bayda crater can be accessed by local Bedouin jeeps. The best views are from Jebel Abiadh (Abyad), but walking is necessary.

Side trip: White Volcanoes viewpoint walk   (3hrs)

White Volcanoes Walk Summary	
Start	Bedouin Camp (1760m)
Finish	Bedouin Camp (1760m)
Distance	approx. 9km (6 miles)
Time	3hrs
Maximum altitude	East Crater (1875m/6150ft)
Transport	Private car

To get right among the white zones of the volcano area, it's really necessary to take a local 4X4 vehicle, as the distances are quite long. It is about 10km in a straight line and much more (maybe 25km) driving to the heart of the area, one way. The local Bedouins might be able to take trekkers if they are not busy with their camels. We have no idea of the cost; it is whatever it's worth to individual visitors! One local jeep driver implied he could take us, but with no way to communicate, we had no idea if this was actually so; no mention of possible cost or timings could be discussed. It would probably take half a day to do it justice using a jeep.

For most visitors without a 4X4, the following hike gives a good overview of the area, albeit further away from the heart of it. There are two viewpoints, with the second one at the rim of the adjacent crater to the east. Be sure to carry extra warm clothes; in winter it can get cold, with bitter winds up here. Don't go without lots of water and snacks. Boots are recommended and walking poles.

The walk begins (going south) just after the first enclosed area to the right on an obvious jeep track. A second settlement to the east has no name, but the Bedouins live there when they are in residence. Follow the jeep track across a flat plain to the lava fields that appear on the right. These flows hide hard-to-find gemstones, according to a local searching the area. There are some great **circular flow** patterns close to the route. The track passes a small **mosque** on the left and begins a steady but easy climb to a house on the right about 40mins from the start. A **Bedouin tent** was seen here. Looking east is the rather undramatic outline of another volcano; it holds a surprise later!

The jeep track climbs more steeply now and taking the track to the right is less steep. This climbs on to a shoulder and soon there is a huge **crater** depression to the right (west), with a great view of **Jebel Qidr**, the dark volcanic cone. It has a couple of dramatic craggy vents on its northern skyline. The track reaches a plateau area overlooking the crater, with great views to the dome-shaped **Jebel Abiadh**, the long creamy-coloured lower **Jebel Bayda** and another steep-sided conical cone to its north with no name.

The first objective is to climb the small hill ahead (south). The last bit is steeper, but the 360° view from the **hilltop** is amazing. (25.71923°N; 39.975133°E).

The contorted dark flows from Jebel Qidr stretch to the base of Jebel Bayda, where the black and white flows meet. There is a great crack in the flow far below, near to the base of the slopes of the viewpoint. It's hard to know if **Jebel al-Aqir**, the hat volcano, is in view, as there are two flat-topped volcanoes to the south. It takes about 1hr 30mins to this viewpoint.

From here head northeast towards the undramatic-looking cone that for convenience could be called **East Crater** volcano, down quite steeply and then up on the jeep track. (25.724412°N; 39.977756°E). It gets ever steeper up to the jagged rocky rim, but the views down are a rewarding surprise. The crater supports yellow grasses that **camels** delight in. We were lucky to see the camels heading up to meet their owner, who had brought ground-up fodder to supplement the grasses. He, of course, could get his jeep up the crater slopes with some skill.

The views of the main volcanoes are impressive, even from this distance, and absolutely fabulous if the skies are crystal clear. It's about 25mins from the viewpoint to the top of the East Crater.

The return trip is faster, and it is possible to take a direct track down on the west side of the East Crater, heading back to the road in 45mins.

Be sure to check for nasties like scorpions if sitting for a rest on the lava flow. The large cone seen to the north from here has distinct red colouring and is just one of many cones that dot the region.

The sealed road continues east for about 15km, with more lava fields and cones. This road is scheduled to be built to Al Hayt (Hait), which will be about 62km from the Bedouin Camp area, and a good link to the notable rock art at Shuwaymis.

Shuwaymis

About 200km northeast of Madinah is Shuwaymis in southwest Ha'il province; it is particularly noted for its rock art. This part of the Arabian Peninsula experienced a much wetter climate in the past, possibly between the 10th and 7th millenniums BC. The rock art and engravings illustrate the fact that wild animals roamed the region and were subject to hunting activities. The lava flows of the **Harrat Rahat** nearby reached to within 4km of Madinah in 1256AD. Other lava outpourings flowed to the east and are also near Shuwaymis.

Jebel al-Manjoor and Raat

The rock art at Jebel al-Manjoor and Raat (Rat) has been dated to 10,000 years ago, making them some of the oldest such sites in the country. There are wild ass, cheetahs, leopards, packs of dogs, bovine images, hunters, and even a hunter with a lion (at al-Manjoor). More recent images show camels and even horses. When the road east from Khaybar is completed, these areas will be a bit closer to the more visited sites of the region.

East of the Harrat Khaybar is the **Harrat Ithnayn**. The lava flowed here around 3 million years ago, with more recent activity 45,000 years ago, and perhaps even as recently as 1500 years ago.

White Volcanoes – Madinah (3hrs)   230km
The route is described earlier going north. It's about 1hr back to Al Thamad from the volcanoes, and 2hrs to Madinah. About 60km before Madinah is a very high massif to the east. For a less tense adventure, stay on or outside the outer ring road.

Madinah – Wabah Crater (3–4hrs)   270km
Madinah is massive and driving around the ring road just outside the Haram area is chaotic. Once clear of the northern intersection flyover (under construction), it's OK, but in all it takes 45km of ring roads to clear the town from west to east.

Dark lava flows and volcanic cones near Madinah

Follow the road (via **Ad Dumayriyah**) southeast from Madinah through the lava fields, small volcanic cones and scoria cones. Leaving the lava flows, the scenery is characterised by plains and low hills until, on the east side, is a chain of peaks including **Jebel Said** and **Jebel Hadb-ash-Sharar**. This range is approximately 140km from the Madinah exit junction.

The scenery is ever bleaker to **Mahd adh Dhahab** (also Al Mahd) about 220km from Madinah. The road joins route 8258 just before Al Mahd. The town is quite large and off the main highway on the east side if a hotel is needed. Continuing more southeast (now on 8454) via **Al Regabiyah**, the scenery is much the same.

About 120km along the road, watch for a communications tower on a **red hill** to the east, just before **Hafir Kishb**.

Look out for the unmarked junction to Wabah (Wa'abah) Crater on the left. (It is marked on the right, if heading north.)

Wabah Crater

Don't expect the crater to 'rise up' out of the plains. It is a mere 2km along the side road to the crater carpark and visitor centre, an elegant stylish new building, which may be closed. There are a few viewing platforms ahead from the carpark, and a black stone wall.

Beyond this is the fabulous sight of the crater dropping below the plains in a near perfect circular, sheer-sided depression that is the crater. The brilliant white of the salt pan is dazzling, with patches of greenery etched into the dark brown walls. The viewing platform on the left (north) has more obscured views than the one on the right, where from a high point there is a clear view down. It gets quite warm here, even in winter.

Side trip: Wabah Crater Walk   (2–3hrs)

It may not be a very long walk, but the heat in the crater bottom is quite stifling and coming back up more demanding when very hot. Good footwear is needed, and sticks preferred. Take plenty of water and snacks in case the trip is longer than planned, either through fatigue or more likely a longer walk on the crater floor.

The trail down is on the north side, some 20–30mins or more around the rim. Those with 4X4 can drive around easily to the starting point. Initially the path is quite steep, and the stones underfoot may roll, so care is needed. The route descends the first small **cliff strata** to the east, where it's broken. There is a short respite before the next cliff, similar in height down and negotiated to the east again, where the cliffs allow passage. Once down this second level, the trail zigzags steeply down to the bottom.

The white **salt pan** – sodium phosphate – is not far ahead.

Wabah – Taif (3hrs)   260km

It's a long, flat drive with increasing vegetation, enlivened by a few towering but distant mountain massifs that look enticing for trekkers.

The route continues across ever more flat featureless plains to join the main Riyadh–Jeddah highway. The flat landscape continues with more low bushes appearing as it approaches Taif.

There is a large fuel station about 90km before Taif.

The vegetation is **Sahel-like** in nature, with low bushes that carpet the sand in green.

Taif

Introduction

The town has long been a retreat for Saudis to get away from the heat of the desert. As the fifth largest city in Saudi Arabia, Taif is set at a cool 1870m in the Sarawat mountains. It has long been known as the city of roses, and despite a population of over 1.3 million, it retains an air of calm once away from the traffic. Its proximity to Makkah has made Taif a pleasant place for pilgrims to rest and enjoy a cooler retreat, away from the holy shrine. The climate allows agriculture to thrive. The rose season is in April, when the fields around are painted in pink. The noted 'damask rose' oil of Taif is used in some well-known perfume products by Chanel and Guerlain.

Taif is normally visited from Jeddah and Makkah. A slower, winding mountain motorway links Taif with Abha, but there are a lot of towns and the road is not a true motorway. Some might consider taking the coast road if time is short, as it's less stressful and faster. The Asir mountains rise up to almost 3000m, so it's a much colder place to visit. In winter snow is possible on the highest ground.

Accommodation

The choice is good, as the town is on the pilgrimage circuit during the Hajj. Randomly chosen by us, the Hotel Venice Towers is on the right of the airport road going into town, next to a number of other hotels, all unmarked in English. Rooms cost from SR130.

Eating

Most of the eating options are fast-food places, with many of the familiar places thrown in here, like MacDonald's and Pizza Hut, as well as Al Baik.

Historical background

Many people of Taif are descendants of the Banu Thaqif tribe, but it is thought that Jews and Ethiopian Christians once lived in the region. Taif was once a walled city and may have been a religious centre for the goddess Al-lat, known as the Lady of Taif.

Johann Ludwig Burckhardt

Perhaps the most famous outsider to visit Taif was Johann Ludwig Burckhardt. The Swiss explorer visited Taif in 1813 and wrote about the city at the time. He apparently met with Muhammad Ali, the nominal viceroy of Egypt, while it was under Ottoman rule. At the time Muhammad Ali had just recaptured the city of Taif for the Ottomans. Burckhardt's records suggest that the city was still in ruins after its sacking in 1802 by rebels allied with the Saud forces. Burckhardt noted that the city walls boasted three gates and a number of towers built by Othman el Medhayfe. The tomb of Abdullah ibn Abbas, an ancestor of the Abbasids, was much damaged. At this time the Thaqif were the major tribe of the city and they traded in coffee.

In 630AD the battle of Hunayn took place close to Taif, as the Muslims encountered resistance from the pagans. With the victory of Islam, the idol of Al-lat was destroyed. Much later the city, along with the Hejaz, fell to the Ottoman Turks before becoming a part of the greater Hejaz controlled by the Hashemite, Hussein bin Ali (also written as Husayn ibn Ali), the Sharif of Makkah.

Along with much of the country, in 1926 Taif fell under the control of Abdul Aziz Al Saud, who united the whole country as Saudi Arabia in 1932.

The sights

Old Fort

Built by the Ottomans, the fort is some way out of modern Taif and closer to the site of an ancient souk that pre-dates Islam. Apparently, some basalt stonework remains here also. We did not get to either on our limited itinerary.

Sharif history museum
Some visitors have enjoyed this place and consider it one of the better museums to visit.

Shubra Palace
Rarely open, the high black and white building has four storeys and is the regional museum and government building. It dates from around 1900 and in 1930 was used by Abdul Aziz al-Saud. King Faisal also used it for his council of ministers. It's on a busy road on the way out of Taif on the east side of the road to the south, and worth a quick detour despite the traffic.

Shubra Palace

Al Rudaf Park
The park lies south of town and is characterised by ancient granite rocks, where the trees seek out spaces between them.

Wadi Mitna
Pilgrims sometimes visit Wadi Mitna close to Taif. This is said to be where Muhammad took refuge in 619AD and where he then tried to enlist the Hawazeen and Tawfiq clans to his cause, without success at first.

Al Hada Nature Reserve and Ash Shafa
The Al Hada, meaning place of tranquillity, hosts trees and plants at around 2100m, making it a cool retreat. Al Hada is northwest of Taif on the way to Makkah along route 15 (45). Ash Shafa village, southwest of town, is even higher in the mountains at 2400m, and is a fertile agricultural area producing mainly fruit.

Taif – Jeddah (2–3hrs)   **190km**
This route completes the northern circle option; we did not do all of this, but headed south from Taif directly to Abha.

The route follows the **5th ring road** around Makkah to avoid the holy city. Look out for the viewpoint of the imposing **Clock Tower** from over 16km away at the end of Ibrahim Al Khalil Road. See under Southern Region below for more details.

Makkah (Mecca)

Introduction
As the most holy centre for Islam, non-Muslims **cannot enter** the city. The 5th ring road around the city has **very clear signs** informing non-Muslims where they cannot or must not go. This section is mentioned here because of its significance, and for the historic background that is essential in any guide to the country.

Accommodation
Non-Muslims cannot enter the city. Muslims will find plenty of choice on hotel booking websites.

Eating
Non-Muslims cannot enter the city.

Historical background
The history of Makkah (possibly once called Bakkah) according to Islam dates back to Abraham (Ibrahim) and his oldest son Ismail, who built the Kaaba around 2000BC. The Kaaba was probably a shrine for pagan tribes in the 5th century, whose deity was Hubai.

This was probably the case until the 7th century when Makkah rose to fame as the birthplace of Muhammad (pbuh) and the place of his first revelations.

In the 5th century, Makkah was controlled by the Quraysh, who were traders along the overland spice trade route; a route used to avoid pirates in the Red Sea. Another trade route to Persia was originally threatened by the Sassanids, who later protected the city from attacks by the Axumites of Ethiopia. Makkah eclipsed both Petra and Palmyra in trade at this time. The Persian king, Khosrau, prevented Arabia from falling into the hands of the Christians around the time that the Prophet was growing up.

Makkah's prominence was due to its well (Zamzam) that sustained life in the barren desert, and because it was at a crossroads for trade. The well itself was a sacred spot for pagans, being so important to habitation. Ptolemy mentioned the city of Macoraba in his work 'Guide to Geography', proving that 'Mecca' was known to the Hellenistic world.

Muhammad was born in 570AD into a Hashemite faction of the Quraysh tribe in a cave on Jebel al-Nour, according to Islamic tradition. In 610 the Prophet Muhammad (pbuh) began receiving divine revelations from God through Archangel Jibra'il (Gabriel); some occurred in a cave on Mount Hira. He preached Islam against the paganism of the people of Makkah, but was forced to flee with his followers, the Muslims, to Madinah in 622 (known as the *hijrah*). The conflict between the rest of the Quraysh and the Muslims continued. In the 624 Battle of Uhud, neither side triumphed.

It was not until 627 in the 30-day Battle of the Trench (also called Ghazwa Khandaq) at Madinah that the forces of Islam became more powerful. In 628 they returned to Makkah, but were blocked by the Quraysh. The Treaty of Hudaybiyyah allowed a tense peace, but it was violated by the Quraysh after two years. The superior forces of Islam marched on Makkah and peace ensued. The city became the holiest site of Islam and Muhammad (pbuh) returned to Madinah, where he died in 632.

Makkah retained its status as a holy site, despite the shifting of power by Ali, the fourth Caliph, to Kufa. The Omayyads then centred on Damascus, while the Abbasids chose Baghdad. Makkah again rode to power under Abd Allah ibn al-Zubayr.

The Omayyads besieged the city in 683 and 692, but it remained governed by the Hashemite sharifs. In 930 an Ismaili sect sacked the city, but the city remained a pilgrimage centre as the holiest site for Muslims. The Ottomans held sway from 1517. Thereafter the history of Makkah is the same as for the rest of the country.

The sights

As mentioned, the main sight for pilgrims is the holiest place of Islam. At its core is the Kaaba, a large black cube. Everyday thousands of pilgrims circle the great shrine in observance of Umrah.

Since non-Muslims cannot enter the city, the only way to get any appreciation of the famous shrine city is from the 5th Ring Road outside the forbidden Haram area.

Amazingly one can see the top of the incredible building that looks over the holy site from the road between Jeddah and Taif. It's quite a scenic drive around the southern ring road, as the mountains and desert have a rugged grandeur. See details under the route description section Qunfudhah – Jeddah via Makkah (ring road).

The Hajj

The Hajj (meaning pilgrimage) is held in the twelfth Muslim lunar month of Dhu al-Hijjah. The Hajj has become a world event each year, as millions of Muslims descend on Makkah. Pilgrims come from across the Muslim world, from rich and poor countries. Every Muslim is expected to make the pilgrimage at least once in their lifetime. Pilgrims circle the Kaaba, getting ever closer to the sacred stone. One of the most important parts of the Hajj is to drink from the sacred Zamzam well and then go to Mount Arafat. The pilgrims spend a day on the mountain to pray to Allah for forgiveness of their sins and to ask for strength for the future. Mount Arafat is where the Prophet Muhammad (pbuh) delivered his farewell sermon to the Muslims who followed him on the Hajj. After the rituals at Arafat end at sunset, the pilgrims move to Muzdalifak for the Maghrib Prayer and the Isha Prayer before taking a rest.

The Umrah is recommended in the Quran and performed at the Al Haram Grand Mosque in Makkah all year. The Jeddah Hajj airport terminal is always busy with Umrah pilgrims.

Al Haram – Grand Mosque

Absolutely off-limits to non-Muslims, the mosque must be a fabulous sight. Non-Muslims can see pictures of it and watch the television broadcasts of the pilgrims circling the Kaaba. It is the largest mosque in the world.

Abraj Al-Bait

Known as the Abraj Al-Bait (Towers of the House), this vast complex contains seven hotels and is owned by the government. The Clock Tower is the third tallest building in the world and the clock face is the world's largest. It's also the world's most expensive building, said to have cost $15 billion, and sits on the former site of the Aiyad Fort, an Ottoman structure from the 18th century. It overlooks the Grand Mosque.

Alternative routes:

Northern Red Sea Coast

As we suggested earlier, the choice of routes and how to lay them out in this book is tricky. From Wadi Qaraqir and Tabuk, the route described above headed east to Tayma, Khaybar and to Taif, but there are also hidden treasures in the Sarawat mountains along the Red Sea coast to explore.

There are a couple of alternative routes between the northern places, such as Duba, Wadi Qaraqir and Madinah. The more interesting option is to visit Al Ula first and then head south through the mountains and lava fields via Al Ays and Yanbu, to Madinah (for Wabah Crater and the southern Asir region) or to Jeddah via the coast. The easiest way south from Wadi Qaraqir to Jeddah is along the coast via Duba, Al Wajh and Yanbu.

Duba – Jeddah (2–3 days)   825km

Those who like the sea air can follow the coast road. In fact this route could eventually be started at the Jordan/Saudi border if it opens. Parts are already described above, through Al Bada to Aynunah and south to Duba. We did not drive the section between Al Wajh and Yanbu. The stage to Yanbu – Jeddah is outlined below.

Duba – Al Ula via Al Wajh (5–6hrs)   400km

The road south (route 55) is fast and quiet along the coast to Al Wajh, with desolate scenery and glimpses of the Red Sea. To the east are distant mountains; generally the terrain consists of rolling brown hills.

About half way to Al Wajh there is a sign for **Zafar mountain** to the right, although there are just more rolling brown humps and dips on view. Just before Al Wajh there is a fuel station that just might have rooms above the shops. It takes about 1hr 45mins to cover the 155km to Al Wajh from Duba.

Al Wajh

Al Wajh is a pleasant town with the turquoise sea lapping at its shoreline and garden-like corniche. Historically there is little to get excited about, but it is no extra distance to divert along the seafront. Hotels overlooking the sea include Hotel Masal Wajh, Wajh Beach Hotel and then Rkaez Apartments.

The road from Al Wajh heads inland for Al Ula, going northeast through wild countryside with a few isolated camel farms and small oases. One of these is **Al Gazazza**, with a small wadi surrounded by balmy palms. Not very far along, and closer to the central ranges, is **Al Beda**, with a fuel station and a 2km long line of decorated balls set in superbly colourful flower beds with real and artificial grass. All very strange, unless it's planned to become a much bigger town in future.

Getting off this narrow road for a tea break is almost impossible, except where the old road is seen on the right, about 65km before Al Ula. The route continues to **Al Balata**, with no fuel, and a line of red flat-topped cliffs keeps the road companion for most of the way to Al Mogayra and the turnoff north for Al Ula. For more on Al Ula and Mada'in Salih, see page 115.

This completes the alternative stages along the Red Sea coast from Tabuk to Al Bada, Duba and Al Wajh (and then inland to Al Ula).

Al Ula – Yanbu – Jeddah

Al Ula – Al Ays (3hrs)   245km
For those with time and looking for a wilder ride back from Al Ula to Jeddah, this route might fit the bill. It's well off any tourist route, but not without interest. This option goes via Al Ays and Suq Suwayq to Yanbu, and then along the Red Sea coast to Jeddah via Rabigh.

From Al Ula the route heads south towards the airport and then south again at the junction before the airport. Very soon on the left (east) is a small **lonely fort** looking for some attention from the restoration agencies. The valley south is quite fertile, with small palmeries below dark brown and black forbidding hills.

The narrow road follows the **Wadi al Jizi** for some distance; there are warnings about flash floods with a dam at one point to control the water. After 100km, a side road is marked to Madinah, but it's not sure if it's a good route. The main settlement en route to Al Ays is **Murraba**, a small community.

Al Ays and Harrat Lunayyir
Al Ays is a slightly confusing settlement, with the town divided by a small ridge. The main area is on the west side of this barrier. There are two apartment-style places listed here, Remas and Saavani, if you need a place, but finding the man with the key may take time.

Just south of town on the route to Umm Lajj before Al Fera, 2–3km from Al Ays are the amazing **lava fields** of the **Harrat Lunayyir** not to be missed even if it's just a quick glimpse from the road. In any case, walking into this rubble maze is not recommended.

Just after the lava flows are lost to view, there is a dirt track off to the right which, according to Google Earth, leads to a small crater-like feature. It is around 4–5km to walk around on the track and we cannot guarantee that it's worth it. This track circles the depression and comes around to a small tarmac side road that rejoins the main road. We could not do this in our small car.

The palmeries are extensive and dates are sold on the

roadside. This area is **Al Fera**, 10km from Al Ays.

Geologists may want to try walking out to a couple of other crater-like feature/cinder cones, visible on Google Earth, and tell us what we missed! It could be quite a long hike, as the terrain is fissured, unstable and potentially dangerous without a local guide.

The power of nature

In May 2009 a strong earthquake hit the volcanic area of the Harrat Lunayyir near Al Ays. The quakes created an 8km-long fracture on the surface. In three months, over 30,000 earthquakes were recorded and 30,000 residents were evacuated. Vulcanologists interpreted the events as being due to a shallow intrusion that did not reach the surface. This event was defined as a volcanic earthquake swarm. In this case the swarm was characterised by both low and high frequency earthquake activity, where the usual gas and explosions were absent. Subsequent investigations decided that the earthquakes were volcanic in nature, with intrusions at a shallow level; part of volcanic seismic activity. At least three cinder cones are found poking up from the contorted lava fields. See https://volcano.si.edu/volcano.cfm for more detail and aerial pictures

Lava flows and cinder cones near Al Ays

Al Ays – Rabigh via Yanbu (4–4½hrs)   335km

The pleasant town of Rabigh is home to the acclaimed King Abdul Aziz University and a lagoon or two along the coast. It makes a good, easy stopover on the long, desolate coastal run to Jeddah.

There is no need to go back to Al Ays (also Al Eis and Al Eis), as there is a link road through some wild hills back to the main road for **Yanbu** and Suq Suwayq. Another road goes east to Madinah here. There is a quirky sign proclaiming the 'End of the DUEL road' – but with so little traffic that's a misnomer. It's another lonely ride to Suq Suwayq; the amazingly sheer and rugged mass of **Jebel Radwa** on the west side of the road is a big distraction. The

mountains withdraw steadily before **Suq Suwayq**, where there are some significant mud ruins and a lot of dead palms to observe from the road. From here the wide wadi is dotted with the remains of a number of evidently once significant mud settlements.

Ruins of Suq Suwayq

The wadi widens much more and soon the **highway** between Jeddah and Yanbu is reached. The vast industrial area of **Yanbu** probably holds no interest for tourists, other than a few beach resorts further north. We did not check this area.

Heading south, the six-lane highway is only of interest because of the number of slow, old trucks than ply its smooth surface. The plains are wide here, with the sea and mountains quite distant. It's a fast road with speed cameras.

Rabigh

Rabigh is a pleasant town with fresh sea air, away from the heavy traffic around Jeddah. There are no obvious sights other than the undeveloped lagoon coastline. Hotel Rabigh Tower is a gem of a place to stay and could be a posh version of a hotel in Dhaka. The Bangladeshi staff are friendly, and the rooms are pretty good for the price, from SR180 including breakfast. It has a good value restaurant too – such a rarity at a hotel. The nearby mosque comes with melodic calls to prayer. The Rabigh Park Hotel nearby is twice the price.

Rabigh – Jeddah (2–3hrs)   170km

The motorway is flat and straight; the only variable is the traffic in Jeddah. The motorway gets ever busier after **Thuwal** and it's around

2hrs to the airport area. From there it's anyone's guess how long it will take through the northern areas to town (Al Balad).

Rabigh – Taif (3–4hrs)   315km

Anyone heading back to Riyadh will need to take this route and bypass Makkah. The road passes under the new high-speed train line to Madinah and then gets lost in the maze of mountains north of Makkah. A 37km sector of this northern **Makkah bypass** is not a dual carriageway; with hundreds of heavy lorries it's a bit of a nightmare drive. The southern option is better but longer, offering the chance to glimpse the Abraj Al-Bait tower in Makkah.

It's a fast 70km run to the **Thuwal** junction, which is slightly confusing since the signs do mark Thuwal, but do not mark either Madinah or Makkah. About 9km along the road is the turn-off for Makkah, which links to the northern bypass. Around 45km from the Makkah junction on the right, and smack in the middle of a complicated crossroads, are the substantial remains of the **Usfan Pilgrims Fortress**, a stone-built structure. Parking is impossible and snatching a photo out of the window not much better. The route continues south–southwest and then east following the Makkah road. About 28km along is another junction where non-Muslims need to continue northeast around the holy city. This road actually goes someway north, not just to avoid Makkah but also some quite high mountains with many lightly inhabited wadis between them.

After 25km this loop becomes a rough, **unkempt** single carriageway, with hundreds of trucks also bypassing Makkah. Most of the trucks go very slowly and some enjoy getting very close to small cars! The surface is rough with some speed bumps, probably because a new highway is under construction on this missing link. The single carriageway continues for 37km and then, oh joy, a new motorway leads on to **Al Sa'il Al Kabir** and the **Al Bahytar National Park** on the left. Great and small outcrops of granite boulders dot the landscape, but we have no idea what other gems the park holds. From here it's another 20km to **Al Muraysiyah**, where the delightful Diafat Almasif apartment hotel is found near the fuel station on a bend. There are shops, café and food available in the street. It cost SR100 for a two-roomed apartment with TV, fridge, sofas, good beds, shower and a squat toilet – well, nothing is perfect!

Just along from here is the **Dreams Inn** hotel on the left, another possibility. Heading for **Taif** it is another 20km to the edge of town, where the other cheaper hotels are found.

See Taif (page 173) for details and **Southern region** (page 211) for routes to Abha.

Central Saudi Arabia

Introduction

For simplicity we describe the northeast central route between Riyadh and Tabuk, that includes the three provinces of Qassim, Ha'il and Al Jawf, in this section. This region has historic mud cities, forts, oases, rock art, rugged outcrops, deserts and vast sand dunes, enough to enthral any visitor.

Some of the road journeys across the region are relatively flat, with featureless landscapes, but others have dramatic cliffs, purple mountains and endless sand dunes. The long stretches on the route might need to be interrupted by some coffee breaks to keep the driver awake! The towns of Buraydah and Shaqra are no longer the small settlements seen in 1974 by Bob. Ha'il is a large settlement further north and Al Jawf, including Dumat al-Jandal and Sakaka, is a surprisingly massive conurbation.

Map of Central Saudi Arabia

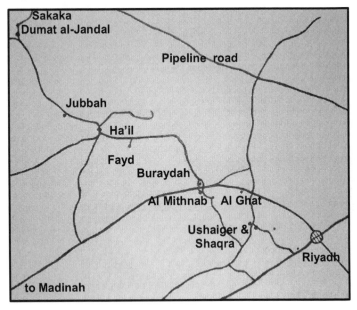

Jebel Tuwayq

Jebel Tuwayq is a very long escarpment that crosses much of Saudi Arabia, from the Najd upland region almost to the Yemen border. It is up to 600m high in a few places, more than 800km long and dates to the Jurassic period. It's a major geographical feature of the country, with the central zone running quite close to Riyadh.

Riyadh (Diriyah) – Shaqra (2½–3hrs)   **195km**

It is with some relief that the chaotic traffic of Riyadh is left behind. Avoid the motorway route and take this scenic drive for much of the way to Shaqra. The road descends the Jebel Tuwayq escarpment to the historic remains of Marak (Marat or Marah) just before Shaqra.

Coming from Diriyah, the outer ring road crosses a number of small canyons and valleys as it circles for 10km or so to the main road junction for Jeddah and Makkah. The traffic is dense until the suburbs are left behind. About 30km from Diriyah, the road suddenly descends the dramatic cliffs and outcrops of the **Tuwayq Escarpment**.

Shortly afterwards go right at the juction – it's marked to Shaqra along route 505, about 150km from here. There are views east of the escarpment cliffs, with small clumps of greenery before superb red dunes obscure the ridgeline. These dunes are part of the Urayq Al-Bildan. Camel farms and small palmeries can be seen to the east. The road is mostly good, with a few potholes nearer the sides.

Marak is a small settlement with some crumbling mud remains

seen on the south (left side). It's definitely worth stopping here to see the picturesque fort with its quaint defensive towers. The local warden is very helpful; he explained that the well seen here is over 1500 years old and was discovered by traders going to Yemen. It looks like a new hotel is being made ready on the left going out of town before the road bends around! It is about 40km to Shaqra.

Shaqra is a pleasant stop with open desert views. Just off the southern ring road (on the southwest side before leaving town) go right to find the green Hotel Asfar on the right (it's advertised by the hotel booking websites). A double room costs SR200–220 but could be less.

We paid SR180 including breakfast on a quiet day. It's a superb clean, modern place and highly recommended.

Old Shaqra

The quiet and pleasant mud remains of old Shaqra are north of the modern area near King Fahd park. An arch heralds arrival here, with the **Al Saibai Palace** on the right, a mud structure that is likely to be closed. Along the road 100m or so is an entrance way into a more substantial mud city. The **mosque** and minaret face a courtyard with quaint houses, walls and a well. The area is surrounded by palm trees and an inviting ambience; it's well worth a short stop.

Shaqra – Ushaiger (30mins)   **20km**

From the old city, head back south briefly and take a road on the left, it's signposted to Ushaiger along route 50 in a northwesterly direction. Follow the brown signs for Ushaiger. The old mud town is on the east side of the settlement off route 50.

Above: Historic Shaqra. Below: Ushaiger

Ushaiger historic settlement

Introduction

The fabulous historic settlement of Ushaiger is a highlight of the region. It is one of the best preserved and renovated mud cities in the country. Currently it is possible to drive in through the entry gate; so far there is no entrance fee. The following is the route we stumbled around in awe, but in truth there are a lot of other alleys, tumble-down remains and gardens in the whole area. The main tribe of the area are the Tamim.

History

As one of the oldest towns of the Najd, Ushaiger was once called A'ekel. Being along the pilgrim route from Iraq to Makkah, it gained importance far beyond its own setting. Bedouins first came to Ushaiger before the pilgrims and exploited the springs, the palms and the agricultural richness of the site. Today it is commonly known as the 'small blonde', after the nearby red mountain.

The sights

From the main roadway entrance, just around the corner is an ornate building on the right and the private **Al Salem Museum**, which charges SR10 to enter. There are a series of alcoves and rooms, hosting household goods, weapons, guns, implements and a mass of other local collections.

Almost opposite is **Al Naswan House** and next to it the larger, more modern-styled **Al Mathaf House**. It has a vast hall on the right with some old photos and other items of interest in alcoves. The owner is very friendly and offered us tea. Heading right, there is an open area to the right with two lanes to it. Here it's easy to photograph the buildings (restored and ruined) and note a colourfully painted door. Back to the junction is the **Mahasin market,** but it's not obvious where the stalls would have been set up here. The Grand Hamad Resort sign claims that food and drinks can be had nearby.

Going left from here leads to **Abdulaziz Alsalem son's house** with two lanes each side. Going right here leads to the **Dar Alhumaid Heritage museum**, which might well be closed. The **Governor's House** is close by. Continuing on leads out to the gardens and palm trees on the east side of the complex. Going left from the 'son's house is the **1st School** and around on the right is the **Abdulaziz-Abdullah-Abdulaziz Al-Shenaiber House**. Try saying that after driving through Riyadh!

Near here is the **Fulaigiyeh mosque** with a small minaret and courtyard through an elaborate doorway. Another junction is ahead.

Ushaiger old city: Fulaigiyeh mosque

Going right leads to **Al Omar House**, although it's not obvious which one it is. At the next junction, going right heads out to the gardens and palm trees again. Following the left path leads around to a **deep well** with some intricate doorways nearby. Continuing in an anti-clockwise direction, pass the **North Mosque** before coming back to the main square adjacent to Al Naswan House. Before leaving, take a look at the **May Door** down the alley beside the museum.

Ushaiger – Buraydah (3–3½hrs)   320km

Once on to the main Riyadh–Buraydah/Qassim road, the traffic is very busy and there are many slow trucks in the inside lane. Signs mark the Buraydah/Unaizah (Unayzah) conurbation as Qassim.

From Ushaiger the road heads due north, with red sand dunes and the lower escarpment in view. Follow this road towards Al Maima'ha for around 50km to meet the main motorway (route 35) from Riyadh. Take the motorway for around 25km to find a layby services area with a MacDonalds/Sama restaurant. If a bed is needed, just along from here a motel is advertised on the right. The turnoff for **Al Ghat** old town is here. Go south from the motorway and once down the steep hill and cliffs of the escarpment at a roundabout go left towards the palmeries for 2km or so to find the sites.

The motorway continues to Qassim/Buraydah, but the city could be hectic, as it's mainly a business centre.

Al Ghat (Al Gat)

Nowhere near as extensive as Ushaiger, the remains of Al Ghat are still worthwhile if time is no object. The ancient houses are set on the slopes to the north, interspersed with a few more modern buildings. On the right (south) is the palmerie, with some restored structures, a well and a mosque.

The name of Al Ghat is said to have originated from the noise or echos of the waters rushing through the canyon. Renovation work is ongoing and it's a slow process making mud brricks from sand, straw and water. There is a shortage of the acacia wood that was originally used. The museum building is worth a look, but may not be open.

Camp en route to Buraydah in 1974

Ar Rabadha

The almost unknown site of Ar Rabadha is not really en route to anywhere, nor between any major centres, so it is included here.

Around 200km east of Madinah, Ar Rabadha is an early Islamic city located on the pilgrimage route between Al Kufa in Iraq and Makkah. Excavations have revealed a well-developed city, with large houses, huge fortified walls, watchtowers and the remains of mosques.

Qassim province

Buraydah

Introduction
Buraydah is the capital of Qassim province and, despite its desert location, is a considerable agricultural centre. It has the largest date palmeries in the world, which also produce oranges and lemons. Dates are harvested in August–September. Surprisingly, with irrigation, wheat also grows here. Buraydah has an airport and was a vital oasis on the pilgrimage routes from Baghdad to Makkah.

Getting there
Buraydah is a day's drive from Riyadh but at least two days from Jeddah. There are SAPTCO buses. From Tabuk it's a long drive, 2 or 3 days. The airport connects with Egypt and the Gulf States as well as domestically to the main cities. By road it is 320km from Riyadh and 250km from Ha'il. The new SAR railway links it with Riyadh and Ha'il.

Accommodation
As usual, check the major booking websites, which are normally more up-to-date than any guidebook. **Note** that there are no accommodation options listed on the east side ring road, so if it's a bed that's needed, head into the fray of the city.

Eating
There was nothing obvious in 1974, but it's a massive town now! Every conceivable brand of fast food and chicken-and-chips can be found. Be sure to buy a good stock of fruit and food from the supermarkets for any journey north especially, as it's remote.

Historical background
The history of Buraydah is linked to the pre-Islamic trade routes that get scant mention indirectly through the poems about the regions water sources before the coming of Islam. The oasis lies on the Zubeida route (named after the wife of Harun Al Rashid) that allowed pilgrims to travel between Kufa (in Iraq) to Makkah. Buraydah owes its beginnings to Rashid Al Duraiby in the late 16th century. He was the leader of the Al Abu Olayan dynasty from the Banu Tamim tribes.

From that time the city and greater region of Qassim was fought over. The Al Sulaim ruled for a while, and then Muhanna Salih Aba al-Khail took power, but was defeated in 1890 by the Rashids from Ha'il. In 1904 Aba al-Khail again established power, until the region became integrated into Saudi Arabia. A treaty still allows the Al Sulaim to govern nearby Unaizah.

Escarpments on the road between Riyadh and Buraydah

The sights

There are a few historic sites in Qassim/Buraydah, but some patience may be required with the traffic if using it as a base for excursions.

Qassim Museum

The museum building is a massive and impressive structure in its own right. It houses a wide variety of artefacts and has displays to keep history buffs immersed for a few hours.

Markets

The date markets might be of interest to those with a sweet tooth. The palmeries of Buraydah are said to be the world's largest date-producing area and there is a date festival to add to the interest. The town is also quite famous for its camel markets.

Mithnab

The traditional village of Mithnab is around 25km southeast of Unaizah off the ring road. It has been completely restored and is similar in style to Ushaiger. There are almost 400 houses within the 2km square area. Allow half a day to visit Mithnab from Buraydah. With a major issue with the Buraydah traffic, we sadly we missed this place. Those on public transport will need to negotiate a taxi.

Al Shinanah Tower

Located east of Buraydah, this 27m-tall brick structure, looking like a slender minaret, is a watch tower, probably over 200 years old and part of other fortifications. It is situated in a region that was at the centre of the Ottoman–Arab conflict. Some of the hostilities between the Al Saud and the Al Rashid occurred here. It is near Ar Ras, one of the main towns of Qassim province, famed for the poet Hassan bin Thabit who accompanied the Prophet Muhammad (pbuh). We did not get to this place.

Ha'il province

The Ha'il region has a large number of rock art sites, whose subject matter is beyond the scope of this guide. It's a long drive from anywhere to Ha'il and the sites are likely to be of most interest to those who are rock art aficionados. Check out the informative website www.saudi-archaeology.com. The Ha'il city area has three fortresses of note: A'Arif, Barzan and Al Qishlah.

Qassim – Hail (3–4hrs)   295km

Be sure to fill up with fuel before leaving the suburbs of Buraydah; it's an empty quarter for facilities despite the new wide motorway. Fences along the road will deter anyone considering camping in their own campervan.

If accommodation is needed, there are a couple of apartment-style places in **Ar Rawd** (also on some maps Al Jiwa), but finding the man with the key might take time. It is quite a big rural town with new buildings, but apparently no regular hotel. The one on Booking.com is uphill from the central roundabout of town to the east on the right above a shop. The shop man may call the key man. They quoted us SR250, which we declined. North of the main roundabout before a massive mosque complex on the left is another hotel above a shop; a man tried to phone the hotel owner but there was no reply.

Only consider coming to this town if desperate, as it's off the motorway. The fast road continues to the turnoff for the next place of interest – Fayd.

Fayd and Shinan

Fayd is located off Route 65, the highway between Ha'il and Buraydah. The small settlement of Fayd hides a big secret. Excavations have revealed that this now-insignificant place was once an important settlement on the pilgrimage route from Baghdad to Makkah and Madinah. It's a rather arid place – not the typical oasis of one's imagination.

Coming into the settlement from the motorway, there is an elaborate structure on a roundabout and then almost opposite the fuel station/ATM are the remains of the **fort** on the right (west). This area is before the main village.

History

The isolated settlement owes its existence to its underground water supply and its position on the pilgrimage route from Baghdad and Kufa to Makkah. The route to Makkah through Fayd became known as the Darb Zubaydah, and was developed under the founder of Baghdad, the Caliph Abu Jafar al Mansour, and his granddaughter in the 8th century. Much later the explorer Ibn Battuta visited during his famous travels, noting the plentiful water supplies.

The sights

Fayd Fort

Today there are remains of a stone fortress-citadel, a mosque, water systems, a large cistern and a museum. Despite its former importance, the sights today are limited to a fenced enclosure.

The remnants of the fort are not very extensive, but the striking factor is the building materials used. Dark volcanic lava blocks from the nearby Harrat Umm al-Hurruj have been used to build the low walls and ten towers that are spaced along the wall. Inside there are signs indicating a mosque, cisterns, bakeries and other long-gone structures. The signboard here suggests the fort was known as the Kharash Palace. Another tells that on the northern side of the fort there is an octahedral pool called Fisquyah. Despite being a major historical archaeological site, on our visit no one asked for an entry fee and the gate was open – it was a Friday morning!

Going south into the village, the other entrance is 50m right and right again to the white 'Faid antiquities office' building with no remains on view. This road going west will lead to Shinan, where there is a basic hotel; Fayd has nothing but many streetlights, three shops and two parks near a hill to the southwest.

Shinan

Shinan to the northwest is a much larger settlement than Fayd, set below some hills and a dramatic sheer cliff.

Accommodation

There's only one place, as we understand. From Fayd the road heads west and then turns into Shinan. Follow the road northwards to find the main shopping area. There is a Rajhi Bank on the left and then a fuel station on the right. The 'hotel' is on the right after this, behind a courtyard/parking area. Rooms are OK for SR100, with hot water but no sheets (sleeping bags are useful).

Ha'il City

Surrounded by the hills of Jebel Shammar, the city of Ha'il is a pleasant urban area with less frenetic traffic. It is one of the more manageable towns.

Getting there

Ha'il is around 850km from Riyadh via Shaqra and Buraydah, but the roads are excellent. Flights and trains are also available.

Accommodation

As usual, check the major booking websites. There are a number of options for the business community. We stayed in the Raoum Inn on the northwest side near the ring road, because of the ease of driving. Rooms are from SR194. A similar place is 100m south. The views of the Jebel Aja (Aga) are a plus here. As usual there is no restaurant or food on site. The Garden Mall is 1km to the northeast, but surprisingly there is no supermarket here.

Eating
There are the usual fast food options and some more costly restaurants in hotels in town. Those heading north to Al Jawf really do need to stock up, as it's a long and lonely journey. There is a Lulu supermarket on the southwest side of town, where route 70 meets the ring road.

Historical background
Ha'il was a stopover point for pilgrims coming from Mesopotamia and Persia long ago; it was on the trade routes from the valley of the Tigris and Euphrates when camel caravans plied the routes. Later it became a major stopping point for pilgrims from Baghdad and Kufa en route to Madinah and Makkah. As the caravan routes declined in favour of sea routes and later the Hejaz railway, Ha'il too declined. The rivalry between the Al Saud and the Al Rashid from Ha'il played a major role in the history of the country. Ha'il was the capital of the Emirate of the Al Rashid from 1836.

The first Emir was Abdullah bin Rashid, who ruled with his brothers until his death in 1847–8. He continued the construction of the Barzan Palace fort and was succeeded by Talal ibn Abdullah. Under the relatively tolerant Al Rashid, trade flourished and foreign visitors were admitted. These included Lady Blunt, Charles Montagu Doughty and Gertrude Bell. The Al Rashids held power until 1921, when the Al Saud gained control of the country. Ha'il became just another small town in the desert after this. Hatim al Tai was the city's most famous son, a distinguished poet just before the coming of Islam. W. E. Palgrave was the first Englishman to set eyes on Ha'il (and Riyadh) in 1862.

The sights

A'arif Fort
Located on a hill above the city, the A'arif Fort is a must-see spot. It dates from the 17th century and was initiated by the Al Ali clans. The Al Rashid dynasty added to it. The fort is over 40m long and houses a mosque, baths, storage areas and basic facilities for periods to withstand attack. The Laget Lelmedi Athr museum can be seen to the south, with an old car outside.

When the compound and parking is completed it will be a top attraction. Currently the fort is closed but it's possible to walk up the pathways for a superb view over the city. It is located 1km east of the main north-south road in Ha'il.

View over Ha'il city

Ha'il: Qishlah Fort

Annayef Palace in Jubbah

Al Qishlah Fortress

This massive and impressive fortress in Ha'il was constructed in 1940. The walls are over 8m high and there are eight watch towers. Inside, the vast courtyard has 142 surrounding rooms on two levels, with white painted columns. Built in clay, stone and wood, it conforms to the local Najd style. There is a mosque with no obvious minaret and an old Land Rover! Nearby is the modern but stylish central mosque with very high square minarets.

Barzan Palace

Completed under Talal ibn Abdullah, it was once a prominent structure, but was demolished in 1921 by the al Saud. Today little remains.

Ha'il Museum

The Laget Lelmedi Athr Heritage Museum south of the A'arif Fort is located in an old mud structure. It might be possible for those interested in visiting the rock art at Jubbah to request a permit here. (Permits for Jubbah can also apparently be obtained from the Ateeq Naif al-Shammari Palace, the museum in Jubbah).

Historic Mosques of Ha'il

Three historic mosques have been restored in the Hail region. The restoration of some historic Ha'il mosques started with Al-Jarad Mosque; others were the Qafar Mosque and Al-Jal'ud Mosque. All three structures consist of mud and stone walls with wooden roofs. The Al Jarad mosque is located in the historic town of Maghaydah and dates back to 1862. It was restored in 1962. The Qafar Mosque is located in the village of Qafar and dates to the early 19th century. It was founded by Ruqayyah Bint Abdullah after the death of her husband. The mosque was renovated in 1965. It has a rectangular minaret. The Al-Jal'ud Mosque is located southeast of Ha'il in the region of Samira (south of Fayd). It dates back to the eighteenth century and is on the pilgrimage route. It was rebuilt in 1928. See www.arabnews.com for more details.

Jebel (Jibal) Hibran and Jebel Sunaynah

This area of outcrops is located west of Ha'il. There are some unusual formations and a natural arch, all interspersed with sandy areas. It can only really be accessed and appreciated by those with a 4X4. Jebel Sunaynah is another hard to reach area, where spiky granite rocks are surrounded by sandy zones. A local travel agent might be necessary to visit these areas. With our small car we could not possibly go there; certainly, the hire car companies would have been horrified!

Mahajah

Only accessed by 4X4 with an experienced local guide and driver, Mahajah is in the desert off the road (route 70) between Ha'il and Al

Ula, around 200km west of Ha'il. The region hosts stunning natural rock arches that are a rare sight in the country. Part of Jebel Uwayqir, some amazing rock art is located at Hafirat Laqat. One rock wall, over 160m long, hosts countless carvings. There are lifesize horsemen, camels, buffaloes, goats, nondescript shapes, and apparently even an image that looks like a boat! Driving only a Chevrolet Spark, we could not visit.

Ha'il – Jubbah (1–1½hrs)   110kms

Once beyond the northern ring road of the city, the route is northwest on a dual carriageway to meet the main route 65 for Al Jawf (signed as Al Jouf here). Be sure to **fill up before leaving Ha'il** as there are few places en route and none after Jubbah for 250km.

Just before joining the highway around 15km north of town on the west side is a large new fuel station with supermarket, fast food and a hotel. Those coming from Al Jouf might try this to avoid the scrum of town late in the day. Going north, it's necessary to drive north and loop back to get fuel.

Once on the three-lane highway, it's a breeze to the Jubbah turnoff, crossing **vast dunes**. It's amazing to see the six-lane dual carriageway snaking across the vast **An Nefud desert** that took weeks to cross and presented real dangers in days gone by. There are some very deep hollows in the dunes, and some small vegetation clings to life. Traffic is light for such a wide highway, with a few trucks and hardly any laybys. Fences again line much of the route, with the **SAR railway** line to the east on impressive embankments.

Turn off south for Jubbah after passing the oasis of **Rawd**. Downhill is a roundabout and signs for the historic sights going west (right). It's about 10km to the rock art, but before that is the town of **Jubbah**. Oddly the rock art signs stop and are replaced by signs for **Al Naif Palace**. Follow these to see the two 'palaces' – see below.

Jubbah

Many sites of ancient rock art are found in the mountains overlooking Jubbah, almost due east of Tayma and northwest of Ha'il, at the southern edge of the Nefud desert. Some estimates put the age of the rock art as far back as 10,000 years. The art reflects the fact that thousands of years ago the area was characterised by wetlands and marshes. There are images of people, depicting their style of clothing and how they hunted. Some of the rock carvings date from around 5500BC.

There are two sights in the town of Jubbah, the **Al Naif Palace** and the **Annayef Palace**, both in the northern area before reaching the rock art sites. Both are currently undergoing restoration.

Al Naif Palace

This was a bit of a building site in Jan 2020, but there is a well and the private palace is being rebuilt. A café is also being finished in the shady garden area. A fee of SR10 per person is charged.

Annayef Palace

This palace just north of the Al Naif is a curious-looking place, with pancake-layered towers and heavily restored walls. It's not currently open. There is a large mosque with a tall minaret close by and ablution block for worshippers (and other visitors).

Rock Art sites

For the rock art, go uphill from the palaces and turn left then right up on to a wider open road above the oasis. Continue heading west towards the massive mountain area of the Jebel Umm Sinman, with some amazing outcrops. There are two areas here. A small fenced enclosure is uphill straight ahead; other more extensive areas are located along the main escarpment to the left.

Jubbah lookout & small enclosure

The first enclosure is not likely to be open, but there is a great view over the area from the car park. The outcrops are sure to be home to some rock art, but it's impossible to see without a local guide. A nearby nomad tent is the guardian's place when in residence.

Rock Art

There are three main periods of rock art at Jubbah. The oldest, dating to 10,000BC, belong to the Neolithic era and can be seen as human figures in all styles. The Chalcolithic period is represented by animals in general; these images are dated 6000–5500BC. The more recent Thamudic inscriptions can be traced to around 3000BC. The images at Jubbah give an insight into the lifestyles of the people and their social status. Other images give clues about hunting techniques. The images date as far back as 9000 years to the period known as the pottery Neolithic era. One visitor of note was Lady Ann Blunt, the daughter of Byron, who came with her husband in 1879.

> Jubbah is one of the most curious places in the world, and to my mind one of the most beautiful.
> **Lady Anne Blunt**

Main escarpment

Head back down the hill and turn right to find the major art sites. There was no charge here for us, visiting on a Saturday before noon. It may all change soon. Set below the soaring mountains and among some impressive sandstone outcrops in the sand are a stunning collection of ancient images and petroglyphs.

Jubbah: access to the art

The King

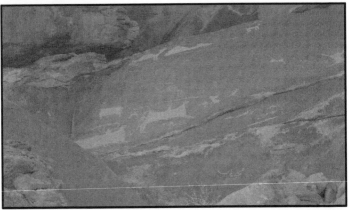

Jubbah rock art

Neolithic man and cow petroglyph at Jubbah

Northern group

From the gate, head along a walkway under a metal structure to the yellow walkway staircase. There are a couple of images up here; one engraving, said to be the **King**, looks like a man with a crown. The other has a halo-like pattern above an indistinct figure. Heading anti-clockwise, there are some simple images of **camels** followed by more **animals** on the northeast side. Around to the northwest side, it's the outcrops that are impressive.

Camel images

Some of the best images are seen high up on the west side. There are some large square images of animals and what appeared to be **men on horseback** carrying long spears. **Ostriches** are visible here. Continue around to a second yellow ladder. This area is amazing, with **camels**, men on camels and Thamudic/Nabatean **script**, maybe a **lion** with a long tail and an engraving of a **tall thin man** holding a boomerang-like tool. A **buffalo/cow** is on his left.

Southern group

Heading south to the outcrops near the entrance, go left from the yellow ladder. At first there is little but the amazing sculptures of nature (of the outcrops) and then through a gap are more **camels**. There is a damaged engraving of an animal with long legs and no head. Then higher up are more camels and **scripts**. Camels with **long necks** are among the concluding images before returning to the gate. Apparently there are horses and chariots somewhere on the Jubbah site, which we did not see.

Rock art at Jubbah

Outcrops at Jubbah hide some secrets

Other areas

From this area drive south along the cliffs, where a vast area is closed off by fencing. This was not open and could be the area that requires prior arrangements to visit. Humans, oryx, ibex, gazelle and cattle are also found in the region, indicating a wetter climate. The following detail comes from www.researchgate.net: Four sites close by are **Jebel Katefeh, Jebel Qattar,** and **Jebel Gattar A & B**, with ostrich images. UNESCO recognised these sites in 2015.

Far North region

Al Jawf province

The northernmost province of Al Jawf (Al Jouf) is a long way from the major attractions of the country. Close to Jordan and Iraq, it is noted mainly for its remote desert landscapes and the oil pipeline road to the Gulf. It's described here within a long loop from Riyadh via Buraydah and Ha'il to Tabuk.

Don't take the wrong road!

Those who manage to get to Al Jawf province, from whichever direction taken, can visit the mud remains of the forts, wells and defensive structures along one trade route from Baghdad. Neolithic rock art and other ancient remains on a limited scale can be found in the area. Al Jawf, like Qassim to the south, is a general name for various settlements; here they are Dumat al-Jandal and Sakaka.

Jubbah – Al Jawf (2–2½hrs)   280km
Crossing the sandy wastes of the **An-Nefud** is an exciting trip that once took weeks by camel caravans en route to Madinah for trade and pilgrimage. Currently there's no fuel or facilities this far from 'civilisation'. It is potentially remote, but the feeling is diminished due to the impact of the motorway snaking through the dunes.

From the Jubbah rock art site, it's easier to continue south briefly from the vast enclosed area south of the main area and go left (east). This road is quiet and passes some of the **large**

circular irrigated agricultural areas. Be sure to turn left (north) to regain the highway signed to Al Jouf, passing a roundabout with a sculpture of a dune with a jeep on top. It's adjacent to a fuel station – **the last for 250km** thus far, although some are under construction near Al Jawf.

The desert route (65/35) continues, crossing vast dunes with more hollows. It's a lonely drive with scant traffic. The railway stays close on the east side and there are a few places to get off the road, more so if it's a 4X4 your driving. There are fewer fences on the side nearer Al Jawf. Just before Al Jawf turn left, following the signs for Dumat al-Jandal, to join route 80.

Follow signs for Dumat (Dawmat) and drop into the town with palmeries to the northeast. At the roundabout, the antiquities are to the right and a good hotel to the left.

Dumat al-Jandal

Introduction
Considering the remote location of Al Jawf today, it comes as a surprise that so much history is attached to the region. Yet another oasis on the trade routes, its history can be traced back over 4000 years. Neolithic remains are found here, as well as ancient castles, citadels and mud cities. The main settlement of Al Jawf (Al Jouf) is Sakaka, with Dumat al-Jandal a separate town. Dumat is spelt on signs as Dawmat, Domat and other variants.

Map of Al Jawf Area

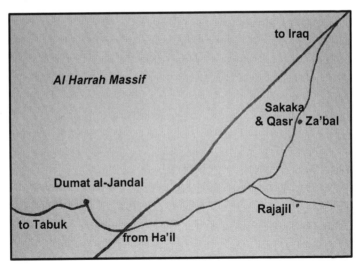

Accommodation

The Admato Hotel is hidden behind some apartments (more expensive) and a car showroom about 1km from the roundabout. It charges SR190 for spacious rooms with the usual fridge, TV, AC etc. It's SR130 for a smaller room with no lounge.

Eating

Dumat al-Jandal has all the usual fast (or fat) food places, including a Kudu branch near the main entry roundabout. There is a good choice of coffee places around town.

History

The Al Jawf region has long been a crossroads for trade as the main northern centre, located between Mesopotamia, the Hejaz and the Arabian Gulf. According to texts from the Assyrian era, Middle Eastern caravans crossed the deserts of northern Arabia via the oasis of Al Jawf and Tayma on their way south to Yemen. At that time Dumat al-Jandal was known as Adummat. Dumat al-Jandal was part of the Nabatean empire in the 1st century BC until the Roman takeover, when it joined the lands of Arabia Petrea under Petra.

The strategic location of the oasis allowed it to retain its prominence as a trading centre, which both Pliny the Elder and Ptolemy noted during the 2nd century AD. Trade was conducted as far away as Byzantium. Being so close to the Middle East, the history of the Al Jawf region is closely intertwined with the subsequent empires and dynasties following the demise of the Nabateans. It fell to Islam during the Caliphs and then became part of the domains of the Omayyads. It was also incorporated into the Ottoman empire much later, until it became part of Saudi Arabia.

Records from the 19th century suggest that the oasis had a series of circular walled enclosures known as suqs. These small, secure enclosures housed the populations in mud brick structures, with spaces for camels and market squares. A village elder or sheikh ruled each settlement under a regional grand sheikh. The enclosures were separated by palmeries and gardens.

The sights

Dumat al-Jandal

The oasis of Dumat al-Jandal hosts a couple of amazing sights as well as the 2.5km city walls that remain. Qasr Marid Castle-Citadel and the Omar Ibn al-Khattab mosque are the main sights; they add up to a very impressive spectacle. Currently entry is free to all areas.

Qasr Marid Citadel

Overlooking the oasis on a limestone cliff is the Qasr Marid Citadel, which means 'the rebel' in Arabic. It is thought to date back to the Nabatean period or probably earlier.

Marid Castle is on the right on entering the car park area. It's a drama-filled, soaring structure with one wall that appears on the verge of collapse. A gateway leads into a large compound on the right, surrounded by walls, turrets and some buildings. A small alley on the left leads a deep well.

Most visitors will want to climb up the winding stairway for a fabulous view of the mosque and old stone city below. The steps are quite steep, but not too daunting. The pathway leads around to the top of the castle, with views across the old city and far beyond into the oasis. There is a small diameter well up here, with no sign of the water far below in its dark depths. The open area at the top offers views of the turrets, battlements and some mud structures.

Marid and Queen Zenobia

The most famous historic incident at the castle was in the 3rd century, when Queen Zenobia of Palmyra (in modern Syria) invaded the city (along with Taymar) but was unable to penetrate the fortress. In failing to enter the castle the Queen is said to have shouted 'Tamrrad-marid'. The name Marid has since been associated with all that is impossible or rebellious. Parts of the structure can be traced back to the Nabatean period, others to after the coming of Islam.

Omar Ibn al-Khattab Mosque

Some scholars believe the mosque was first built under the auspices of the Caliph Omar Ibn Al-Khattab after his return from Jerusalem. Others suggest it was really constructed by the Omayyads some time between 661–749AD. It's a striking sight, with the five levels of the minaret catching the eye. The mosque sees a constant stream of domestic visitors, such is its grandeur. Probably the mosque was once within the massive walls of the oasis, some of which remain today, and which probably date to the Nabatean era. The minaret, 12.7m high, is one of the oldest in Arabia. A notable feature of the mosque is its floor plan, which conforms to early Islamic styles. The meaning of 'Jandal' relates to the stonework.

It is still surrounded by mud and stone-built houses, with walled alleyways lending it an air of the exotic. The **mosque** can be entered down steps beside the iconic minaret. It's a spacious area with many columns and a simple area for worshippers. Steps lead up the minaret, but it's already leaning to one side!

Omar Ibn al-Khattab Mosque

The old city
The old city spreads out into the palmerie from the mosque. To the left the houses are mostly in ruins, but there is an alley beside the minaret leading into some impressive walled lanes through archways and tunnel-like corridors. There is a deep well out the back near the palm trees, and over to the northeast corner there is a great view of the castle, mosque and turrets.

Al Dir'e District
We did not visit this area, but it too apparently has the typical stonework of the region.

Dumat al-Jandal – Sakaka (1hr)   60km
Leaving Dumat the motorway heads east through arid plains decorated with lines of power pylons! A line of low cliffs to the north shelters the ancient oasis.

Those looking to visit **Rajajil** might find the access road blocked with roadworks. There seems to be another way to get to it, which we did not actually follow, as the road didn't look finished either. See more on Rajajil below. The main road turns northeast and reaches **Qarah**, which is really joined to Sakaka. Qarah is about 45km from Dumat with the Hotel An-Andalous on the right if needed (no prices sorry).

Sakaka

The vast modern conurbation of greater Sakaka (Sakakah) comes as a bit of a surprise to romantics looking for the old Arabia, but the traffic is fairly traditional! It's with some relief that the antiquities are signposted and soon found. There is a small car park below the Qasr Za'bal (Zab'al Fort), with a superb café called **Taaleel** in a garden with water wheels.

Café Taaleel

Don't miss this place, even if it's only for a coffee. The food is great, as is the coffee, and there is an inside atmospheric tented eating area with high or low seating. Simple dishes of hummus, labneh, omelettes, chips, foul and more, with most dishes costing SR10. The café is a popular spot for local people, and during our visit the younger women were insistent on taking selfies with us in the picture. The friendly staff were mainly from the Philippines, with others from Nepal and India.

Café Taaleel

Qasr Za'bal

Standing above some wild outcrops, a small palm grove and the inevitable modern buildings, the Qasr Za'bal of Sakaka is nonetheless a dramatic sight. The ancient site might have been connected to the Nabateans, although the current structure is around 200 years old. Before exploring the fort, it is worth a few minutes walking around the base of the outcrop near the Café Taaleel. There are a couple of narrow alleys and a short stairway for a view. To enter the fort, it is necessary to take a walk around clockwise along the road outside, and then make a couple of right turns going uphill around new houses and a few palm trees.

The fort area is fenced, but currently no fees are levied. Steps lead up to the top, with great views of the city and surroundings in all directions. The top is dominated by several round turrets with small windows that offer more views over the city. There is a closed central building within this fort area that collected water.

Once down, continue around clockwise across the open area (a future parking place) and down to regain the road that leads back to the Taaleel café and car park. To the west of the castle is some rock art and engravings, but these are unlikely to be open to the public.

Sisra Well

Also called Bi'r Saysara, Sisra Well is located about 200m south/southwest of the Qasr along the same road used initially to circle around the fort. The well is believed to date back to the Nabatean period. A rough path leads up to some steps beside an empty triclinium hollowed out of the outcrop. The well is ahead and it's very impressive. There is an ancient stairway inside the well that leads around 15m down to the bottom. Although unseen, on the eastern side is a canal that used to let water out to the ancient city; it is some way down the walls.

Rajajil

Rajajil is a strange site, still under investigation and probably a very ancient place. There are apparently small stones standing in isolation. They are probably part of burial sites and could be as much as 6000–7000 years old. As mentioned, we could not get access in February 2020.

On the road to Tabuk

Al Jawf – Tabuk (4–4½hrs)   415km

It's a great drive for desert lovers, with a real feel of the remote. There are no fuel stations on the southbound carriageway and even those on the other side looked as if they might be closed. Allow 4hrs driving time, plus extra time for heavy traffic in Tabuk.

Beginning from Dumat al-Jandal, the route is on highway 50 west to the junction with the road to **Al Qurayyat** and the Jordanian border. Initially the scenery is flat and bleak, but after the above junction there are high dunes to the south. With no fencing, access to the desert for camping is much easier for campervans and those so equipped.

Later there are low hills and barren plains of shattered rock, with outcrops and black or brown hills to the north where sand clings to the slopes. About 230km from Dumat there is a **bad section** of road for 10km, needing a much slower speed of 70km and occasionally less where it's very rough. There are very few cars on the road, but quite a lot of fuel trucks in small convoys. About 250km from Dumat is the tiny settlement of

Fajar with a fuel station, and again the road surface is rough for a few kilometres.

A kilometre south of the junction with the **Tabuk–Tayma** road (route 45) there is the **Sasco services** with a fuel station, supermarket, closed restaurant and 10 rooms behind if the man with the key can be found. It's OK to cross the central reservation here for those heading from Dumat to Tabuk; a new flyover is being built at the junction. The last 115km are soon done, although the westbound carriageway is rough in places. And so to the large but generally well laid out modern city of **Tabuk**.

See page 146 for details of Tabuk province and Tabuk.

This concludes the routes, historical sights, places of interest, desert scenery and details on the drive/accommodation etc from Riyadh to Tabuk.

A different type of traveller who visited some of the region described was Gertrude Bell.

Gertrude Bell

Gertrud Margaret Bell was born in 1868 and became a writer, traveller and later a political officer. It was as an archaeologist that she travelled to the Middle East and Arabia. She explored Arabia during an expedition in 1913-14 in the footsteps of Charles Montagu Doughty, taking many of the photographs that have appeared in more recent publications of Arabia Deserta. As a woman she was able to enter the Haram of Madinah. Her experiences in the Arab world lead her to become an amazingly influential player in the region. Like T.E. Lawrence she also aided the Hashemites in Jordan and Arabia and also served in Iraq. Her influence and knowledge of the tribes of the region became legendary as she worked in Basra and Baghdad for the colonial powers. during the formation of the modern state that became Iraq. Her extraordinary talents became legendary and was far ahead of her time being a woman of influence in the Arab world. She died in 1926.

Southern region

Southwest Mountains

The southwest region is completely different from the northern deserts, with populated mountains and much more greenery. The terrain is rugged, mountainous, harsh in part and climatically anomalous.

Asir, Bahah and Jizan provinces

Map of Southern region

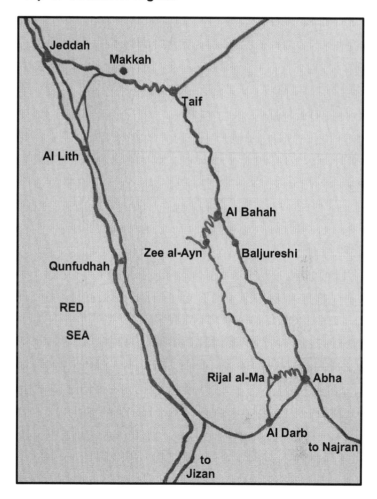

Taif – Al Bahah (2–3hrs) 230km

The route from Taif to Abha is a bit of a shock, after the empty roads of the northern deserts. There are far more towns and thus far more crazy traffic. Some of the towns like Al Bahah (Baha) seem to stretch along the ridges for ages – in fact about 45km – and the 'motorway' has many traffic lights. It's much slower going on this route. Fog can be an issue on the road nearer to Al Bahah (and further south) as it drifts up from the Red Sea mid-mornings, especially in winter.

Leaving Taif the road heads east and for a couple of hours it's not that busy. The mountains are always in view, with some outcrops and spires to the west for the first part. The terrain is still quite dry, although bushes and trees cover some slopes. The road passes through **Al Shoqsan** on route 15 (marked 45 locally). There are a couple of stone villages en route; one is to the west below the road, another is called **Sahhat**. After about 180km, it's on the approach to Al Bahah that the volume of vehicles slows things and nervous tension rises!

Al Bahah

The city of Al Bahah is the main town of Bahah Province; it lies at an altitude of over 2100m. It is noted for its green surroundings, pleasant climate and as a transport hub. Al Bahah has a museum that details the history of the town and region; it also has a noted market on Tuesdays. Picturesque old houses dot the area as well as the Qasabas, which appear to be watch towers or even granaries.

This resort town sits on the main communications artery along the ridgeline of the Asir Mountains. If you need a quick coffee break, duck off the road to the Golden Tulip (SR450 for a room though, so a bit pricey). It's on the right, close to the junction for Zee al-Ayn. We arrived in thick fog and could hardly see the entrance to the hotel; the Turkish coffee was great but the cappuccino machine was out of order!

Zee al-Ayn

Locally Zee al-Ayn is also written Zee al-Ain, Dhi Ain or Tee Ain on the signs that exist. Zee al-Ayn is south of Al Bahah town along Route 246, which continues to Al Makhwah and the coastal town of Al Muzaylif. Also along this route is the junction with the hilly 'touristic' Route 211 south to reach Rijal al-Ma.

This historic village is set on a hill in the mountains, dramatically located on a steep-sided ridge commanding a panoramic view across the hills. The stone houses seem to grow up the hill, with high ridges as a backdrop.

Getting there

Al Bahah lies at about 2100m and Zee al-Ayn is at 800m, so expect a massive change in altitude and temperature. The route drops immediately from the west side of Al Bahah near the Golden Tulip Hotel, which is on the right. The road is astonishing as it descends through tunnels and across bridges around the steep-sided rocky and green hillside. Some of the cliffs are almost sheer and it must have been an engineering feat of massive proportions to carve out this route. It's around 27km and takes 30mins to reach Zee al-Ayn. There are a few laybys, with great views over the massive ravine and the road snaking down. The local driving standards make this excursion a bit adventurous!

Zee al-Ayn village

Driving down after the twisting stage, it is easy to miss the turnoff for Zee al-Ayn, as there is no sign for it going south. It's hidden to the left in a cleft in the cliffs behind a hill up through a few houses. It's a staggering vision of stone houses, fortified summit and gleaming white marble outcrops. All this is set below towering mountains and above a lush green garden oasis of palm trees and vegetation.

Currently the entry office area is not completed, and no charges are imposed. Expect this to change soon. Access to the village is along a stone paved path and the houses soar above this. Steep stairways and narrow alleys characterise the village. It could take an hour or more to explore here, as the height gain must be 100m or so to the top structures. Allow 30–35mins to drive back up to Al Bahah. Be prepared for cars to appear on the wrong side and to cut corners.

Jibal Mussala Ibrahim

These massive granite peaks and outcrops are stunning and can be viewed from the road nearby. They are located 50km from Zee al-Ayn and rise to 2220m, of which 1700m is visible from base to summit. A small sealed road goes to the village of **Sheda**, with superb views en route. This road, however, is better suited to 4X4s. Sheda lies at around 1600m. Ancient dwellings here utilised the naturally hollowed-out outcrops and stonework to make shelters. The drive up to Sheda is of note; the vegetation changes dramatically from top to bottom. Some plants are said to be akin to those found on the Yemeni island of Socotra.

To reach Jibal Mussala Ibrahim the route goes south from Zee al-Ayn towards Al Makhwah and then turns off to the northwest (right) before Al Makhwah.

Baljureshi

Around 25km south of Al Bahah, Baljureshi is a more manageable place to stay. The area between Al Bahah and Baljureshi is less built-up, but the town is quite large and definitely no longer a village. Close to town is the high viewpoint of Jebel Heznah, overlooking the town as well as over the escarpment. Try the Mera Houses hotel on the west side of town: Rooms from SR150 plus tax (SR10). Other places are the Saf Hotel on the way in and the Baljureshi Palace in town. The expensive Swiss International Park Hotel is on the road south out of town.

Baljureshi – Abha (5–6hrs)   380km

From Baljureshi the road is a lot less busy, and there are long open stretches. There are still some small towns to watch out for and the speed limits vary a lot en route. The larger settlements appear to have hotel/apartment-style places to stay. Monkeys have fun causing affrays across the hilly areas, hoping for food scraps from passing drivers. They can be aggressive, so beware!

The road (highway 15) heads east and about 60km from Al Bahah the road negotiates a **massive canyon** where the road drops steeply down before a spectacular climb back up.

After **Sabt al Alayah** the countryside is drier for a while, but later the hills again attract fog banks. There are some wild rocky peaks to the southeast. Further south the lower hills are topped by housing, as are the valleys between. A few impressive **fortress-like** houses can be seen, often hemmed in by more modern houses. Some are in stone, others crenulated and others painted white. Sad-looking **watch towers** blend in with the wild outcrops.

The town of **Ash Shaykh** (2hrs from Baljureshi) has a couple of OK hotels. One is opposite the big mosque on the hill before the main area. It's set in a quadrangle of shops in a newish building. Rooms from SR100. Another down the hill and off to the left (east) is the apartment-style 'Sultan' marked in English. Nobody was manning it when we visited.

From Ash Shaykh the road passes a few old stone villages some mixed with the modern houses, others a little more untouched. About 1hr south of Ash Shaykh there is a massive deep canyon; part of the escarpment. The mornings tend to be crystal clear on the high ridgeline of this escarpment.

It's hard to average much more than 60km per hour along this whole stage to Abha. The road passes through **Al Salamah**, **Bani Amir** and **Al Qahtan** but they are not signed in English on

entry. Further on **Al Namas** is a larger town. About 1hr 15mins from Ash Shaykh there are some impressive rocky peaks and outcrops of Jebel Mana. Possibly made of granite, there are great smooth slabs, boulders and cliffs. On the west side the outcrops are dramatic.

There are more views west over the escarpment at various points, some with laybys. The route passes through **Billasmar** and continues along the top of escarpment. The countryside gets gradually drier and soon there are more traditional old houses; some are white, others in brown stone. Look out for the white tower and house on the left (160km from Ash Shaykh). Off to the right quite soon are the first good examples of the crenelated houses with the typical Asiri lined upper levels. See picture below under Abha.

Asir: white mountain houses

215

Asir: stone house

About 60km from Abha is **Al Zaid**, where the countryside is dotted with slender watch towers. The road heads east away from the escarpment through drier countryside. Further east is the desert, with rugged hills and outcrops on the horizon. The road drops into **Abha**, set in a vast bowl surrounded by dry hills and mountains. It's about 4hrs to Abha from Ash Shaykh and around 6hrs from Baljureshi.

Typical Asiri building style in stone & mud

Abha

Introduction

Abha is the main town of the southern area of the mountains and quite close to the border with Yemen. Lying at a height of 2200m, it is the highest city and 6th largest in Saudi Arabia. It has two rainy seasons, the usual March to May in common with the rest of the country, plus it is reached by the monsoon from the Indian subcontinent in July and August. The Romans called this area Arabia Felix, the land north of the Queen of Sheba's domain and the regions of Himyar. The area was regained from the Ottoman Turks and then controlled by Abdul-Aziz al Saud. In 1934 the 'Treaty of Taif' was signed between Saudi Arabia and Yemen.

Set between 2200–2400m, it has a pleasant climate. It's a good base to explore the surrounding hills and villages, and perhaps **if it's permitted or safe**, the most southerly town of Jizan adjacent to Yemen. The picture-postcard settlement of Rijal al-Ma is about 55km by road from Abha. The contrast between the locality of Abha, which is almost akin to the Mediterranean climate, and the harsh deserts of the rest of the country, is quite marked. Abha has suffered a few security issues related to the Yemen conflict, so check websites for information.

Getting there

Abha airport lies some 15km east of the city. Flights link Abha with Riyadh, Jeddah, Dammam and Taif, plus Dubai and Sharjah. From Jeddah it's a long hot drive along the Tihama coastal road. This route avoids the twisting mountain roads and takes around 6–7hrs. It goes via Al Lith and through Al Qunfudhah, then loops inland to Ad Darb on Route 55, where Route 10 heads northeast into the mountains. Route 15 runs south from Taif via Al Bahah, but it's a tiring drive on twisting good roads through towns with speed bumps and erratic drivers. It is scenic in many parts; beware when driving through the fog. Allow 2 days from Taif to Abha.

Accommodation

The choice in the town is quite varied. Check the usual booking websites or get advice from the locals about other options. Try the La Fontaine Sarat Abha with rooms for SR130–150, on the west side of town on the road to Rijal al-Ma. There is an Oyo at the entry to town coming from Al Bahah. For a spot of luxury, try the superb Hotel Azd down beside the wadi in the centre. Rooms are not cheap, but it's very switched on for tourists. There is a helpful English-speaking travel desk – Tahlal Tours. Mrs Sharifa is extremely helpful, as is the reception desk. For any help call them on +966553195211. Email: ahmed_azd_hotel123@hotmail.com.

Eating

Being a major city, Abha has a fair choice of restaurants and cafés to keep the gremlins at bay. The restaurant at the Azd is excellent for a splurge. Some of the international fast-food outlets are in town.

Historical background

Abha was another settlement that serviced traders and later pilgrims on the frankincense route from the south, Oman and Yemen to Makkah and northwards. Much of its history is linked with the greater area of the south of the country, close to Yemen.

The sights

Abha is not that big on sights, but the mountain views from various places near town are very different from the rest of the country. The town is surprisingly pleasant, with many modern but stylish Asiri traditional-style buildings. With peaks of the **Sarawat mountains** up to 3000m around the area, the setting is magnificent, but with it come some flooding issues. The town has a dam that gives it protection against flash floods. This offers a general view over the town, and the lake provides a pleasant retreat with good facilities for tourists. For a feel of old Arabia, be sure to visit the Al Basta area.

Al Basta

The Al Basta area is part of the original town; it has some colourful old houses of note, with amazing designs. The upper levels have slates in rows, giving a startling appearance above the quaint streets. The restored Alqabel Ottoman bridge is 32m long and 6m wide. It's easy to locate if you find the Hotel Azd – walk south over the road bridge then turn west along the wadi, passing a small recreational park to reach the Ottoman bridge, 100m on the right. The old area of houses and quaint mosque is directly ahead from the Ottoman bridge. Despite being so central, it is not marked on Google Maps.

Museums

The new **Asir museum** just opened is fronted by an Asiri-style house constructed in the traditional style of the region below an impressive mosque with tall minarets. It houses artefacts from the region and describes the various periods in history. There are some typical clothing items and old guns of note. Currently it's free for entry. The amazing architecture of the Asiri building style is eye-catching. One information board explains the 'musnad' alphabet that formed the earliest Arabian writing. It had 29 characters, no vowels and five branches, of which the Thamudic version was one.

Al Muftaha (Miftaha) museum is styled in the white, brown and blue of some of the Asiri houses of the region; it hosts arts and crafts of the area and is located on the west side of town near the dam area.

Abha Ottoman bridge

Modern Abha

Road to Rijal al-Ma

Shada Palace
The Shada Palace is apparently an iconic, high-rise building, constructed in 1927 for the Emir of Asir. It is now a museum hosting items of daily usage. Despite being in the vicinity, we did not find this place. Locals just pointed to an impressive modern building on a plaza across from the Asiri Museum. It could be near the dam close to the Muftaha museum?

Shamasan Fort
Overlooking the north of town, Shamasan Fort is a quite extensive stone structure built by the Ottomans. It is very hard to find, so ask in the Hotel Azd if you are keen to see it.

Jebel al-Akhdar
On a clear day, it's hard to beat the panoramic viewpoint of Jebel al-Akhdar (2340m). It is a great viewpoint for the city and the dramatic mountains around it. It's to the south of Abha and has a café at the summit.

Asir National Park
This park lies southwest of Abha on the edge of the city. It is well watered by the usual rainy season as well as the Indian monsoon. It is close to the lake and dam. There are views over Abha from here.

Near Abha
For those with plenty of time in the region, there are a couple of sights to explore.

Al Souda
This cliff-hugging trip is by cable car from Souda National Park complex about 28km from Abha at 3015m. It gets mixed reviews on the various websites. Apparently it costs around SR80 for the ride, which we did not do, as it was closed.

Jerash
This sight, 30km from Abha, is of interest to archaeologists. The people of Jerash were heavily involved in the battles for Islam.

Moshebah Hills
The Moshebah Hills are relatively verdant and the climate is similar to that of the Mediterranean. We did not visit.

Jebel Sawdah
Jebel Sawdah is the highest point in the Sarawat mountains, part of the Sahab Park at 2900m. It's on the route to Rijal al-Ma, on the south side of the road. With the surrounding plateau region already at a high altitude, the sense of height is not pronounced. Jebel Sawdah is not accessible but can be seen from various points close by.

Abha – Rijal al-Ma (1hr)   **55km**

See below for details of the exciting road journey!

Rijal al-Ma

Introduction

Rijal al-Ma is astonishing. Looking not unlike the tower houses of Saada and Sana'a in Yemen to the south, the ancient Asiri village of Rijal al-Ma is located west of Abha. Here the houses are constructed of dark stone rather than the mud of Saada (and of Najran in southern Saudi Arabia). Rijal al-Ma sits above the dry river on the old trade route to Yemen. The stunning backdrop of the Asir escarpment adds to the ambience. Rijal al-Ma is being considered as a possible UNESCO site. Watch towers, other defensive structures and tower houses dot the area.

The settlement consists of what are locally called fortresses but are really fortified houses on differing levels. There are five and six-storeyed buildings and a mosque. Restoration has been done largely by the local community; they won the prestigious Prince Sultan bin Salman prize for the preservation of Urban Heritage in 2006.

Getting there

By road Rijal al-Ma is 55km from Abha and 170km from Jizan. The road from Abha climbs for 20km to over 3000m before plunging down the escarpment. The turn-off down to Rijal is signed but is quite small. The descent is staggeringly (or horrendously) steep and it twists and turns in an amazing fashion. Be sure to get into **low gear** immediately.

The well-engineered road drops to a first viewpoint of the escarpment. Continuing to snake down, it drops an incredible 1400m in 8–9km from the top turnoff to a large parking and viewing area. Beware of other drivers on this monumentally twisting descent. It's quite possible a small hired car might struggle to get up this steep hill and overheat, so beware. Maybe it's better to go down only and continue to the coast road.

The road is less steep now and comes to the turnoff to the left into Rijal al-Ma; it's well signposted. Those without wheels will have to check options at the Hotel Azd's Tahlal Tours desk. It won't be cheap.

Accommodation

Currently there are no hotels in Rijal al-Ma but a superb new traditional-style building looks like it will be finished soon opposite the site. There were a couple of options down the road about 10km, but we don't know any more than this.

Eating

There is a teahouse at the site, but it was not functioning despite quite a few Saudi tourists arriving later than us. No sign of anywhere to eat or drink in the village, but down the road are food shops by the junction with the route 211. Expect this to change as tourism gets into gear; it's still in **low gear** for now!

Watch towers are common in the Asir region

Historical background

The town was another of those that serviced traders and later pilgrims on the route to Makkah. The townspeople were involved in the Muslim conquests and their exploits were noted by the historian Al Tabari in 636AD; 700 soldiers of the Bariq tribe from Rijal al-Ma and others joined in the battle of Al-Qadisiyah, where Arab fighters vanquished the Sassanids. Some of the population also helped to defend Madinah.

Rijal al-Ma became the capital of the Hala principality in 1331, during the reign of Mossa al-Kenari. In the 18th century the Asiris were involved in the Battle of Besel near Taif against Mohammed Ali Pasha; some refused to leave their comrades until the fallen had died of their wounds. The Swiss explorer Burckhardt records some of the deeds of that time.

In 1822 some of the people of Rijal al-Ma under Saeed bin Maslat rose up against the Ottomans across the Asir and defeated them. In 1828 the Ottomans agreed to the independence of the Asir region after the inhabitants' defiance. However, the Ottoman ruler Ibrahim Pasha did not go lightly, and true independence was not achieved until 1835. Thereafter the Ottoman empire gradually retreated in defeat, as Makkah, Taif and Yemen were fully relinquished.

The sights

Rijal al-Ma complex

The main sights are the various tower houses of the old village that cling to the steep slopes of the hillsides. The houses are all fortified structures with small windows and doorways. This area is also called the Rojal Heritage Village area. Looking at them from left to right, the houses are as follows.

The first lower fortress house is called **Msmar**; it belonged to the Al Alwan family, who traded with places as far away as Aden. The building is over 400 years old. It is now a museum and has five storeys containing various artefacts. Its painted in white and green inside and is very atmospheric. Different rooms have guns, clothing and other items of local interest. Beware of the low doors; entry is at car park level and exit is from the floor below the rooftop level.

Behind the Msmar are the two 'fortress houses' of **Maejib and Hakim** with green windows. The family of Fa'a Ibn Ibrahim al Fa'is, who owned it, had land in Al Darb and Al Sawdah close by; they were traders in grains.

The next building along is the larger **al-Dir'iyyah**, which is more than 300 years old. It belongs to the family of Ibrahim Ibn Ahmad Al-Jaber. The name of al-Dir'iyyah relates to the village scholars of al-Hasaqi, linked to Sheikh Muhammad Abdul Wahab. It was not open; it apparently has frescoes from 1370 painted with dyes from Aden.

Continuing right, the upper building is the fortress house of **al Ssibae** and is owned by the families of Abu Alam, Ben Haider and Al Bakri. It has six floors and its joint owners were traders.

The building in front of the al Ssibae house is the fortress house of **Al Jaber and Al Hawat**. The Al Jaber building is jointly in the ownership of Al Jaber and the Al Raqdi families. Literature here suggests the ownership papers of the house date back to 1187AD. The Al Hawat house belongs to the family of Al Issa-Bin Salem and has 5 levels. This area has a less renovated stairway and the buildings nearby are in disrepair.

Continuing around to the right on the lower level near the teahouse, there is a walkway below some more dilapidated walls. There is a stairway channel/wadi down from around here to the road below the complex.

Currently entry cost SR20 for the two of us.

Turshi Museum
This is located uphill from the main site on the west side. There is a small mosque here with some intriguing decorative stonework. Behind the mosque is a larger building with decorated doorways and more white stonework decoration. There is also a shady superbly decorated teahouse area, but no tea as yet.

Rijal al-Ma village

Southern Red Sea Coast

Jizan
The last major town along the Red Sea before the Yemen border, Jizan (Jezan or Jazan) is not likely to be a popular spot for many foreigners as yet. The coast hosts superb coral reefs and there are inland canyons with verdant growth. Route 55 is the main highway along the coast, the principal artery for all of the southern areas. It was suggested to us that visiting Jizan was OK, but it is quite close to Yemen. The SAPTCO bus runs to Jizan.

Rijal al-Ma – Al Qunfudhah (4–5hrs)   315km
The drama of the escarpment and the superb village of Rijal al-Ma are quickly left behind as the road drops to the humid Red Sea coast of the Tihama. Camels are farmed along here, and the scenery is bleaker, with a few distant views of the hills. Isolated lava flows interrupt the sandy zones. There are more settlements and no issues with fuel or supplies. It's much hotter down on the coastal plains, so keep extra water handy.

The small road out of Rijal al-Ma rejoins route 211 and descends through the valley and gradually opens out on to the **Tihama** plains. There are a few more stone buildings and once clear of the main hills the route is across dry scrub and almost desert. The heat gradually builds up as route 211 joins the main road down from Abha (route 55). This dual carriageway soon reaches the town of **Al Darb** and continues across the plains beside a lot of pylons to the junction with the Jizan (Jazan) and Yemen road (about 150km from Abha).

Views inland along the Tihama coast

Curving north now, the road is faster and the scenery rather dull at first. Later there are more lava fields and blackened hills to the east. Later low dunes appear with various wadis engulfed by greenery – palms, tamarisks and the flat-topped acacias so common in East Africa. There are quite a number of fuel stations, so topping up is not quite so critical.

Heading on north, the road skirts along the Red Sea with small lagoon areas in places. There is a good lunch spot off the road near one of these lagoons at about 225km from Abha on the left. There's no shade anywhere on this road, though. The route passes through a number of towns: **Al Shaqaiq**, **Al Qahma** and **Al Birk**, en route to Al Qunfudhah.

Al Qunfudhah is the largest town so far. It has several hotels and is a local beach resort.

The top place, Alazhar Palace, is under renovation and Sea Village costs SR300+. More affordable are the unmarked Layali Alandlous furnished units for SR150 at weekends, less otherwise. It's on the road to the beach near the Alazhar Palace.

Al Qunfudhah – Jeddah via Makkah (5–6hrs)   460km

From Al Qunfudhah the road continues along the coast across flat plains to **Al Lith**, then heads inland for a diversion via Makkah.

En route there are melon sellers and camel farms, along with some sheep and goat herders. Low sand dunes add some colour and interest, but by now it's the faster, smooth, easy driving road that appeals. After Al Lith there is a side route option for those with time from **Alqalh** along route 304 (on Google maps) and 5 (on maps.me).

We did not follow this road (route 304) but the first stage has some interesting boulder outcrops. We joined this side road (304) later by taking a rougher link road east under power lines that come from the coastal power plants and water salination zone to the west. This cut across country joined the road (route 304) after 24km and then it's another 40km to the route 301 and 3km more to the main Jeddah–Taif road via Makkah.

For curiosity's sake it's worth driving around the 5th Ring Road (route 298) outside the Makkah Haram area for 27km to the wide valley of the **Ibrahim al Khalil road** that gives a view of the incredibly tall skyscraper that overlooks Makkah. The 5th Ring Road continues to Taif, enabling the circuits of the north and south to be visited separately.

Once off the fifth ring road, there are two roads to Jeddah. It takes about 1hr via the Expressway or the older dual carriageway.

A couple of hotel options are found in eastern Jeddah, south of the expressway. These are the Hotel Rawsil and the Al Manzel-al-Hadira (SR150–190 at the weekend). Fast food outlets are nearby. This might save heading into Jeddah in the afternoon rush hour.

Camels along the arid coast

The Empty Quarter

Wander and wonder

We wanderers, ever seeking the lonelier way, begin no day where we have ended another day; and no sunrise finds us where sunset left us. Even while the earth sleeps, we travel. We are the seeds of the tenacious plant, and it is in our ripeness and our fullness of heart that we are given to the wind and are scattered.

Gibran Khalil Gibran, Lebanese poet philosopher

The dunes of Saudi Arabia

Introduction

Known as the Rub al-Khali, the **Empty Quarter** is one of the most inhospitable deserts in the world. It covers an area of 650,000sq.km. and lies in the southern part of the country bordering the countries of Yemen and Oman. It's the largest expanse of sand desert in the world. Much of the area is sand; sand dunes there rise to an altitude of 250m in places.

There are very few oases and settlements. Dried-up lake beds are trapped among the vast dunes, where once hippos and water buffaloes roamed (in the lower Pleistocene period). There are small areas of gravel and luminescent plains of gypsum. The red sand is coloured by its feldspar content. The trading of frankincense was possible by camel caravans across the Rub al-Khali until increasingly arid conditions stopped this around 300AD. The lost city of Ubar (in Oman) was buried by the same desert sands.

Romantic connotations spring to mind; the exploits of Wilfred Thesiger first brought it to the attention of westerners.

Getting there

Access to the region is from Taif to the east and southeast via Wadi Dawasir, from Riyadh via Layla and from the Eastern regions. The only way for tourists and travellers to visit this vast sandy area is with a travel agency experienced in off-road camping expeditions. Most are based in Riyadh.

Accommodation

Self-sufficient camping is the usual way to visit these remote areas.

Eating

Fully supported trips are supplied with food, cooks and equipment.

Historical background

Little is known about the region in earlier times, since there were few trade routes using the desert here. Even today there are only a few oases that can support life.

The sights

A liking for wild places dominated by sand and dunes is the key ingredient here. The silence of the desert night, the whispers of the cool breezes, and the astonishing array of stars are the main attractions of such an adventure. It is amazing to feel so insignificant amid the wonders of nature. The wild, remote sensation of being so isolated is almost calming, and perhaps instils a feeling of awe and even the sense of a greater meaning to life.

Access routes to the Rub al-Khali and Far South

From Taif

Taif/Al Muraysiyah – Ranyah (3–3½hrs)   355km

You might think you have already reached the Empty Quarter on this almost featureless desert run to Ranyah. That said, it's a relief to leave the manic traffic of Makkah and Taif behind. When the new dual carriageway is completed, it might possible to get all the way to Ad Dawasir in one long run.

From Taif it's a question of following the signs for Riyadh, but from Al Muraysiyah the junction is complicated; watch carefully for the correct turnoff – the U-turn is a long way on the road towards Taif! Once on the open road to Riyadh (route 80), it's a good, fast, easy run for about 150km to the turnoff to the right just after **Radwan**.

The desert route is bleak and flat with almost Sahelian scenery of low bushes and a few stunted thorny trees. The next settlement is Al Khurmah, some 65km ahead and reached in under an hour. En route is a sign for the **Mahzat Al Said** Reserve 12km along on the left, although what it hosts is unclear.

There is a wide wadi near **Al Khurmah** and apparently a fort, not found. After this the road falls to bits for 20km as new construction is due. About 90km from the turnoff, the scenery suddenly changes from flat to the lava fields of the **Harrat Nawasif**, with low hillocks of black rocks interspersed with sandy areas. A more interesting area of small cone-like hills are seen on the right in around 35km. The road improves and will be a dual carriageway in a short while, but other than this it's a generally desolate run into the **Asir foothills**. There are **granite boulder** outcrops, low smooth-faced outcrops and distant views of more rugged mountains. A flat-topped massif and a slender tower can be spied just before **Ranyah** – perhaps a place for more exploration if it's not off-limits!

The Ranyah (and Ar Rawdah) settlement has a well-appointed apartment Alfkamh hotel on the right just into town after a fuel station on the same side. It's next to a fast food chicken place and is on Booking.com.

Ranyah is a new town with more hotels likely to be online soon. A fort is marked by Maps.Me, but we did not find it.

Ranyah – Wadi Ad Dawasir (2½–3hrs)   240km

It's a bleak drive across the sands of the Nefud ad Dahi, with no settlements en route and no fuel stations.

Take the route left at the roundabout south of town; it's not marked in English but has a Saudi flag design monument on the roundabout. Leaving the granite outcrops of Ranyah behind, the route crosses sandy tracts with low dunes. There are quite a few distant outcrops and low hills – remnants of the long eroded Asir eastern hills.

The route goes under the direct road between Riyadh and Qal at Bishal. Sandstorms are likely here in late spring and maybe at other times. The road surface is mostly good, but it's only a single carriageway.

The first signs of vegetation mark the beginning of the long conurbation of **Wadi Ad Dawasir**, which seems to be various settlements joined up. The rather functional-looking palmeries are off to the north, so it's not a scenic entry into town. **Fort Barzan** is said to be the only remnant of the historic oasis, apart from the odd mud structure near the palmeries. However, it's not accessible by a small car, as the speed bumps down the lanes to where it is supposed to be are too high! The local kids near the palmeries are not overly friendly either; it is a rural area with no tourism. Perhaps this fort is not worth the effort, wherever it is!

There are quite a few hotels in town, but most are expensive. We stayed at the Ajwa Almsa, apartment-style hotel on the right on the main road going east. It cost SR189 on Booking.com and is a bit posher than most. Eating is the usual fast food and not much to rave about – we had our instant mash and tinned fish as usual.

Wadi Ad Dawasir – Najran (4–5hrs)   410km

As the link to Najran from Jeddah or Riyadh, it is noted here rather than under the Far South below. The historic archaeological site of Qaryat Al Faw is also mentioned here, as it is just off the route south.

From Ad Dawasir the road goes east, passing a sign to a museum on the north side but no indication about what can be seen. Around 40km from town is the **junction** for Najran. With Jebel Tuwayq on the east rising starkly from the desert, the road is a good dual carriageway. About 73km south of the junction is a fuel station adjacent to **Qaryat Al Faw**, a major historic site on the Frankincense route from Yemen.

The sign on the road for Qaryat Al Faw indicates Al Fao, but however it's spelt, it is about 1km off to the east. It's described below in more detail under The Far South, as it's best seen in the afternoon light on **Jebel Tuwayq**.

Continuing south, the route is across flat sandy plains with dunes in the distance to the west. Jebel Tuwayq is often further to the east at times. There's not much of note until a **major fork** junction is reached, where one road continues to

Najran and the other heads southeast to Al Sharawrah. There are a couple of fuel stations and the first on the right has a supermarket and funduq (hotel). This is c.180km from the junction on Route 10/90.

Further south, the next side road is to **Yadmah,** about 40km from the **fork**. Later on, an isolated parking area on the right may offer a rest from the blinding sun and flat sandy plains. There are a few striking **outcrops of Thajar** on the west side – the first signs of the Asir foothills, enough to wake the driver! The long drive continues to the next junction on the right, marked to **Bir Hima** (Hima wells). Hima Wells is described in the Far South section below.

As the road closes in on Najran, the Asir outcrops become more prominent and soon there is a road west to the settlement of **Al Husayniyah**. The suburbs of Najran straggle along the main road for some distance. See below for **Najran**.

Rub al-Khali expeditions

Perhaps the most famous desert in Arabia and the Middle East, the Rub al-Khali is vast. As for the places within the Empty Quarter that can be visited, they depend on the offerings of local travel agencies who organise 4X4 expeditions into the desert. It's fair to say that any trip into the Empty Quarter is only going to touch a tiny part of this vast region. Spending days on end in a purely sand desert is perhaps only for those who want to experience something of the journeys of Wilfred Thesiger. Most visitors probably want 3–5 days in the region.

Various operators offer a 3-day camping expedition from Riyadh, exploring the western side of the desert adjacent to the Sarawat mountains. It begins in the large oasis of Wadi Ad-Dawasir east of Al Bahah, which has a domestic airstrip for easy access from Riyadh, Jeddah and Dammam.

Taking to wheels, the trip heads east in a loop, possibly via the deserted remains of Qaryat Al Faw. The normal route heads into the dunes of the Rub al-Khali before turning northeast. The last stage is on to the settlement of Layla on Route 10, where those with time might get a glimpse of the old mud town remains. From here the road is bleak and featureless for the stage to Hawtat and then back to Riyadh. See travel agencies and tour operators listed in Appendix 5.

Western Rub al-Khali dunes

Wilfred Thesiger

Sir Wilfred Patrick Thesiger was born in 1910 in Addis Ababa, the son of the British consul-general in Ethiopia. He attended Magdalen College at Oxford University, where he read history. He returned to Africa after this and attended the coronation of Ethiopian emperor Haile Selassie in 1930. He then lived in Darfur, Sudan and the Upper Nile region between 1935 and 1940 as a political officer.

He began his journeys of discovery after World War II, going to Arabia when he was sent to investigate plagues of locusts in the south of the country. It was after this time that he crossed the Empty Quarter – the Rub al-Khali desert. He later acquired the nickname of Mubarak bin London. He enlisted the help of the Bedouins on his first crossing of the desert in 1946 from Salalah in Oman, travelling to the Mughshin Oasis before continuing into the sands of the Empty Quarter. Despite some dissent in the company of four guides from two differing tribes, he managed to reach the Liwa Oasis, in what is now the United Arab Emirates.

His second crossing of the desert was in December 1947, beginning at the Al Manwakh wells in Yemen, from where he proceeded to Sulayil in Saudi Arabia. This was without the consent of the king at the time. After a brief imprisonment, he continued to Liwa again and on to Abu Dhabi, arriving in March 1948. He recorded his journey across the Empty Quarter in the book Arabian Sands (1959), in which he laments the impact of oil discoveries on the way of life of the Bedouin. After many other journeys to Asia, in 1990 Thesiger returned to England, where he died in 2003.

Is this the future for the Empty Quarter? Guess where?

The Far South – Yemeni border area

The potential for tourism here is tremendous, but the war in Yemen is not over yet. Yemen, of course, is also a great destination if calm returns. Currently the border region is not considered safe by foreign governments, so readers will have to make their own judgement and take responsibility for themselves if they choose to visit. Ideally find a reputable guide and take local advice. See Appendix 5.

Warning:
Local travel agents in Abha recommend avoiding Najran for now until the war concludes. That is not to say anyone would be stopped on the way. Checkposts might stop tourists, but the official policy is unclear. Your travel insurance may not be valid. Those proposing to visit should clearly accept the risks, which are hard to assess. That said, approaching Najran from Wadi Ad Dawasir is a better option, as the route avoids the border road coming from Abha.

Check the various government travel advisory websites before a visit. The Houthis claim to have raided the Najran border areas as recently as June 2019, although reports are not verified.

Dhahran Al-Janub
Rather too close to the border with Yemen, this settlement between Abha and Najran is best avoided for now. Photographs suggest that some of the houses are like those seen across the Yemen border in Saada. Local advice in Abha suggests it's unwise to visit the town (Dec 2019) due to missile threats and terrorism, maybe even kidnapping.

Najran

Introduction
Najran, lying in the extreme southwest corner of the Rub al-Khali desert, is the fastest growing city in Saudi Arabia. It is a very modern city, but it also has some exotic palmeries, guarded by canyons, wadis and purple-coloured hills. It's extremely close to the Yemeni border and the influence on the architecture is clear. Mud tower houses and fortified dwellings dot the desert wadis.

Getting there
Najran airport lies some 15km east of the city. Expensive flights on Saudia link Najran with Riyadh, Jeddah and Dammam. SAPTCO runs a service to Najran from Jeddah and Riyadh. From Jeddah it's a long hot drive along the Tihama coastal road to Abha and then via Dhahran Al-Janub. This route is best avoided for now. The route via Wadi Ad Dawasir is described above as a route to the Empty Quarter.

Accommodation

Najran is said to be the fastest growing town in Saudi Arabia and the choice of accommodation is quite varied. Check the usual booking websites or get advice from the locals about other options. Hyatt Najran, not part of the Hyatt chain, charges from SR270 upwards, including a hearty breakfast of foul, cheese and lashings of flat bread. There is a cheaper OYO next door.

Eating

Being a major city, Najran has a fair choice of restaurants and cafés to keep the hunger pangs away. Some of the international fast-food outlets are in town. There is said to be a Lulu supermarket west of the Hyatt Najran.

Other

Unlike most places in the country, Najran has an exchange bureau – Bin Yaala Exchange. It's at the junction where Route 15 turns north towards the Park Inn Radisson hotel.

Historical background

Najran was another settlement that grew from the frankincense trade and later the pilgrimage routes from the south, Oman and Yemen, to Makkah and northwards. The city's history can be traced back over 4000 years and it was once known as Ukhdood, which is now an important if little-excavated site near the town. All the trade routes from the southern Yemeni coast came through Najran. The town was conquered in 685BC by King Karibil Watar, a Sabean ruler of Yemen. Another Sabean king, Yithiamar Bayin, routed the settlement in 510BC. Najran continued to be under Sabean rule for some time, and was later ruled by the Minaeans.

Najran was the first Yemeni city to be overrun by the Romans under Aelius Gallus as they headed south to Arabia Felix in 25BC. The city was used as a base for the Romans to attack Marib, east of present-day Sanaa. The Sabean empire collapsed in 280AD after the Himyarites arrived. Perhaps surprisingly, during the 3rd century, the people of Najran chose to align with the Abyssinians before a Himyar king crushed the rebellion.

The city was conquered by northern tribes in 328AD. By the 6th century, Najran was in an alliance with the Axum empire, with a sizeable Christian community in the city. The Jewish king Dhu Newas massacred the Christian and Aksumite communities, burning churches and killing those who refused to denounce Christianity. Much later the Jewish community was exiled to Mesopotamia.

In reality the Yam tribes of Najran wanted neither to be part of Yemen nor Saudi Arabia. Between 1924 and 1932, the Yemeni and Saudi forces fought for control of Najran. Then in 1932 the forces of Imam Yahya of Yemen attacked Najran with more than 50,000 troops.

Most of the people preferred to be part of Saudi Arabia. Under the leading Sheikhs of the Yam tribe, Najran became part of Saudi Arabia in 1934, with ratification in 1937. Najran has a mixed Muslim community with Sunni, Shia and Ismailis.

The sights
The city of Najran is a large and spread out, with the western areas surrounded by beautiful hills; parts are still like the quintessential oasis of a bygone era. Surprisingly there are some extremely fine, decorated tall mud houses set among the modern, mainly in the western suburbs.

Emarah Palace
Located west of the modern city, the Yemeni-style Emarah Palace is a must-see, even though it dates only from 1944. The large fortress-like complex is located in a modern souk area with appropriately styled shop fronts. It covers 625sq.m. and has 65 rooms. Inside there is a mosque and a well, but it was not open.

Al Aan Palace
Overlooking the Wadi Najran on a small outcrop (part of the ridges of the mountains to the north) is the fortified Al Aan Palace, a majestic structure in mud and stone. It was first constructed in 1688 and is also known as the Se'dan Palace. The central building has five storeys; it dominates the complex with white-edged windows set against the mud-coloured walls.

Continuing along the wadi towards Yemen, the road bends south near the Najran Dam and crosses the Wadi Najran on a bridge to pass below the Raum Fort on its southern side.

Raum Fort
Raum Fort is perched high on a rocky outcrop and accessed by a new pathway and stairway of sorts, probably suitable for strong hikers, but we did not have time to check this. Three pools supplied the site with vital supplies. There's not a lot left of the fort, other than the basic walls that encompassed five rooms.

Abu As Su'ud
Abu As Su'ud is a must-see, with superb mud houses and swaying palms set below the rugged hills. There is no specific route around the settlement; ideally ask your hotel for a taxi. Some of the houses have ornately painted crenulated tops, others have decorated windows; some are five stories high while others are falling down. Access is a bit tricky and is best done from the south side down a couple of narrow sealed roads. Just drive in and head to the obvious tall mud houses that dot the area among the palm trees. The people seem friendly, even though a foreigner in a small car is a strange sight, especially for the children!

Typical old houses of Abu As Su'ud

Al Ukhdood

Historically of great significance, the vast enclosed area of Ukhdood does not make so much of a visual impact today. The name of Ukhdood is derived from the expression 'wide and deep ditch over the land'. The site dates to well before the pre-Islamic period. Probably it will be closed, but some remains can be made out through the fencing on the northwest side near the new museum building. When completed, the museum is likely to bring to life the real significance of the actual remains.

Ukhdood (also Ukhdud) dates at least from the 7th century BC and, in its time, was a city to rival those of Egypt or Mesopotamia. There were vast palaces, sizeable merchant houses and, outside the fortified area, several graves, all dating from Byzantine, Umayyad, Abbasid and later periods. Excavations have revealed that, besides the trading activities, Ukhdood was also an agricultural area with dams and canal irrigation systems.

The most famous story of Ukhdood is about 'the people of the ditch', which is recorded in the Quran. The people were thrown into a ditch and set on fire because they would not renounce their beliefs in god (Allah). Various other interpretations of the story have been proffered. A lot of mystery still surrounds the true nature of Ukhdood; further excavations are likely to reveal more surprises, especially as it is so close to Yemen.

Yemeni-style houses: not in Najran but in Saada, Yemen 1987

Further east is **Sharorah** and to its south is **Al Wadiah**, very close to the Yemeni border and on the ancient route to the Hadramawt. The historic and spectacular cities of **Shibam, Tarim** and **Seiyun** were key in the frankincense trade, with links to the mountains north of **Salalah** in Muscat. Much of the frankincense originated in these uplands that rise from the coast along the Gulf of Aden and Mukallah.

Apparently the Hadramawt can now be accessed from Oman, although security issues are a paramount consideration these days!

Najran – As Sulayyil (4–5hrs)   **415km**

The return journey towards Riyadh begins here, but there are a few surprises en route north. Bir Hima is an obvious attraction, but so is Qaryat Al Faw if open. Another surprise is described below.

It's about 40km before the last suburbs of Najran are left behind; soon afterwards is the turnoff for the Al Husayniyah development.

About 90km from central Najran is the turnoff to the west (left) for the Bir Hima wells. It's marked as **A'Abar Hima**; there are U-turn access points about 1km on either side of the turnoff. The narrow but good road crosses sandy tracts and soon the foothills of the eastern Asir appear. It is 22km before a right turn needs to be made. This goes for 4km+ to the first areas of Hima. The new road bends around to the right near a mosque and side road.

Just past the mosque, head left and look for a small tarmac lane with a sandy area at first that appears to block the road. A hundred metres further on is the gate to the **Bir Hima** wells.

The access gate may well be open, as we saw a local water truck filling up here and a friendly repair team were working on the entry area.

Of course, this might have been our lucky day, as an access **permit** to the rock art is normally needed from the Department of Archaeology in Riyadh prior to a visit. Anyone seriously interested in the amazing rock art here should definitely seek the correct entry permits. We did not see any rock art here, as a guide is necessary to fully explore the site. However, the **seven wells** and **picturesque setting** made our trip worthwhile.

Bir Hima Rock Art

The rock art of Hima is spread around a wide area of the foothills in the vicinity of the wells. The closest fenced area to the road is that of Saidah. The art is from the Palaeolithic and Neolithic periods between 2500–1000BC. The petroglyph sights number over 100 and the main images are of humans, giraffes, camels and other animals.

Tools and daggers have also been found here, made of flint, andesite and quartzite. It is thought that the site was a major place of spiritual animism. There are also 6th-century inscriptions linked to the Himyarite king, Dhu Nuwas. There are at least 250 sites west of the wells that those with permits might visit.

As an aside, a significant raid took place in the vicinity of the wells in 518AD. The area was explored by Philby, Ryckmans and Lippen during an expedition in 1951.

Bir Hima wells

Return to the main highway. About 165km from Najran centre, on the west are the Thajar outcrops, where camels are seen in abundance, feasting below the outcrops. The **fork junction** for the road southeast to As Sharawrah and Wuday'ah is next, with fuel, shops and maybe a new hotel under construction.

About 30km north of the big junction on the east side (right) is the extensive **Uruq Bani Ma'arid Reserve** with a good access road that climbs up the dramatic escarpment of Jebel Tuwayq. This place is really on the edge of the true Empty Quarter.

Before coming up here, it is necessary to obtain a booking permit from the Department of Wildlife (Saudi Wildlife Authority SWA) in Riyadh.

The route continues for another 90km or so across the hot plains to **Qaryat Al Faw.** A short 500m sealed road heads off east (right) into the desert. Just to the left of the side road is what looks like a new reception centre. The Al Faw site is directly ahead guarded by a fence and a sign shown below with the phone number for contacting the permit people. We did not try this as our time was short, but a permit will be required for this site from Riyadh in advance.

Qaryat Al Faw

Accommodation

About 1km north of Al Faw is a fuel station with very basic rooms for we think SR15 per bed. These rooms are primarily for truck drivers, but a desperate archaeologist might just be able to stay here as the rooms had AC and local toilet. Bring a sleeping bag for this place.

Curiosity nearly killed the cat

We cruised up to a viewpoint on the road to the Uruq Bani Ma'arid reserve in complete ignorance, wondering what a Saudi reserve was like. Near the top of the escarpment we were met by the reserve staff wanting our permits. Our e-visa was not good enough and we were politely escorted to a luxurious reception tent and complex. After some nervousness on our part, a man who spoke a little English was phoned, and we were offered strong coffee by the four local staff while our situation was sorted out. After a simple conversation using a translation app, a plate of delicious chicken and rice appeared and then some superb local tea. When the chief suggested we wait a little longer, it got a bit concerning. What had we done?

Five minutes later we were escorted to a 4x4, told get our cameras and were driven off into the dunes. Crikey! This joyride was in fact a brief trip into the reserve to see the luxury accommodation in AC tents followed by a quick drive to the fabulous dunes and some very green bushes to scout for birds. Finally we were driven to a more thickly vegetated area and were very lucky to see a deer bounding off. Our short safari concluded back at the base, and now we know what a Saudi Reserve looks like. No dead cats were found here, though. Bird watchers and wildlife enthusiasts should obtain a permit prior to a trip. Contact the Saudi Wildlife Authority in Riyadh.

History

Al Faw was one of the most important 'oases' on the incense routes from Yemen to the Middle East due to its abundant underground water. Unlike most oases, there was and is no vegetation at ground level. The trade in frankincense and myrrh allowed the city to develop from the 4th century BC, as it was on a route from Najran to the Gulf coast. There is evidence that trade also took place as far away as the Levant.

Two sites have been unearthed that seem to imply that the oasis grew in the 3rd century BC as the Minean traders from Yemen enlarged the city. The Mineans worshipped a god called Athtar Wadd. An inscription here suggests that the Lihyans of Dedan were linked to Al Faw. Ties with the Nabateans and the people of Gaza indicate the extent to which trade was prevalent across Arabia. Al Faw was subject to raids by the Sabean and Himyarite powers from Yemen at the end of the 3rd century BC. As sea trade grew, so the overland routes declined, and Al Faw was lost to history.

Sights

From the fence it is possible to make out the main mound of the site. To gain entry it's necessary to contact the department of antiquities in Riyadh. At the site is the following information board which those with a Saudi phone might try to use!

Glimpses of the Al Faw remains

The two main sites at Qaryat Al Faw are the Temple of Shams and the Altar of Aabit, but around twenty wells have been found along with a souk and residential areas. The settlement does not appear to have had any protecting walls. The so-called Tower Tomb outcrops nearby are a strange sight and have burial chambers.

For a great overview of what's on offer, see the website www.saudiarabiatourismguide.com

It's just a short drive north from Al Faw to As Sulayyil.

If the fuel station beds above are not attractive, head on north to the **junction** of the road for Ad Dawasir and go east to As Sulayyil. In theory this road heads through a gorge in the Jebel Tuwayq but the valley is so wide it's not a gorge at all, unless there is a real gorge hidden somewhere on the northern side.

The **Tuwayq escarpment** is impressive on the south side though and the wide valley hosts some attractive palmeries. The route passes through **Tamrah** to the settlement of **As Sulayyil**. Just before town, on the right is the easy to find Al Naif Hotel with a massive parking area in front. It charges SR150 for a good room with everything a traveller needs except food. Bring your own – don't you know this already!

Route to Riyadh

Although not strictly part of the Far South, route 10/90 to Riyadh is described here as a continuation of the journey from Najran.

Layla old town

Unlike many towns, Layla hasn't bulldozed its old city. Located on the east side of town is an extensive patchwork of mud structures, including some that must once have been palaces, forts or rich traders' houses. There is a mosque in the same style on the northeast side of the area and quite a few narrow lanes. Some buildings have the traditional white crenulated tops. The lush palmeries lie further out, east of the old city; there must be a well somewhere here. Hopefully some restoration work will be set up to make this an attraction to see after a trip to the Rub al-Khali dunes.

As Sulayyil – Layla (2–3hrs)   240km

The bleak landscape continues, but don't expect to see any impressive sand dunes along this western side of the Rub al-Khali.

From As Sulayyil the road is good and fast, with almost flat plains and few features. **Qasr Himam** (Hamam) is off to the west, with small palmeries but no Qasr (fort) to be seen. For a while there are dark low hills on both sides on the horizon and **camels** are herded along this stretch. A few small dunes can be seen to the east. The road passes through **Al Badeah** (Al Bad'i) with some palm trees.

After this it's mostly big green circles and farms until **Layla**. Layla is a manageable town, and could be missed, since the signposts for Riyadh take traffic around town on the west side. The central area of town has an elegant clocktower and some quite striking minarets above the buildings.

Tours to the Rub al Khali rejoin the highway here from the east.

Reval Hotel apartments is on the west side of the highway near a fuel station and mosque, tucked in adjacent to both. It's not marked in English. The rooms are SR90–100, so good value and comfortable, as rooms have fridge and western toilets. Bring a towel, as few cheaper places have any.

Old Layla mud remains

Layla – Riyadh (4–5hrs)   320km
The long and not at all winding road (10/90) continues north, with just flat sandy plains for company. We had a sandstorm with wild winds and poor visibility in the morning – a sign of the season and change to hot weather.

There is little to say about the scenery, with only the occasional small hill in sight. The main town en route is **Hawtat Bani Tamim** which is a collective name for the settlements of the area that include Al Hilah and Al Hilwah. Hawtat is signposted as Howtat and Hawtah. On the way into town there are two places to stay for those wanting to avoid the traffic and hotel hunting in Riyadh, if on a late flight the next day. The Narciana is the first on the right; it's a great place with large rooms designed for families and Texas oilmen. Rooms have small cookers in addition to the usual facilities and cost from SR190–200, but are really worth more.

Out of the weekend, we paid a bit less. Just nearby is the Dar Al Asalah for a similar price. About 4km along is the Raoum Inn (SR165).

Hawtat Bani Tamim: Al Hilah Oasis

No one would drive hundreds of kilometres to come here, but if passing with a spare hour or so, it's interesting to visit the palm-filled canyons of the area. There are palmeries set below rugged low cliffs with some ancient mud walls, a few more intact structures, a small hill fort and the quiet ambience of the oasis. It must once have been an oasis of the imagination.

The road heads west at almost the last roundabout going north along the main Riyadh highway. Shortly on the right is a quite extensive, if very dilapidated, former **mud settlement**. Turn left under the road soon and go left along a wide lower **wadi road**. (It's possible to return to the Riyadh highway via a striking cutting off the lower wadi road to the east). There are some less impressive mud remains of what could have been a walled settlement with palm trees all around further along.

Head up right just after this to the larger road going west and cross over to explore the palmeries. Follow your nose north to get to the central area of the modern town with a very impressive **mud-coloured mosque** with two high minarets adjacent to a local produce market. Heading west soon there is a hill with evidence in stone of what was probably a **fort**. Another road further west goes out to the **camel farm** in a small canyon.

On to Riyadh

Continuing north to Riyadh, a new road removes the need to go via **Al Kharj**, although rock art has recently been discovered as well as a 'site' listed on the Michelin map.

After the lifeless plains before Hawtat, the scenery improves, with rolling low **dunes** to the east. Closer to Riyadh are some small wadis where vegetation adds colour. Just before the outer ring road is the wide **Wadi Nesah** and, as the urban sprawl is about to start, there is another wadi and a sign to a lake area.

The road deteriorates just before the ring road and after that so do the driving antics in the congested city. Timings to get around or through Riyadh cannot be assessed, so the time above is to the ring road plus a bit. Those who have time might try to visit **Diriyah**. It cannot be closed forever!

Others with an early flight could try staying at the Almakan Hotel 103 (Mayyum) which on Booking.com might cost around SR136 for a pretty OK room.

It's about 18km from the airport – as close as you can get – on the northern outer area off King Salman Highway.

Eastern region

Az Zahran (Dhahran) and Dammam

Introduction

The large conurbation that is the two towns of Az Zahran (formerly Dhahran) and Dammam is the major oil centre of the country. The massive Saudi Arabian company ARAMCO is prominent in the region. It is currently the focus of attention from investors, as it has been partially sold off by the Saudi government. The operation is the largest share sale on record, raising US$2 trillion.

There is little of interest for tourists in the twin cities, other than the fact that they are the major transport links of the east. Not far along the coast northwards is the causeway that now links the island of Bahrain to the mainland.

In 1974 Bob drove past some of the oilfield flares that illuminated the night sky. The group were invited to stay at a unit of the ARAMCO oil compound for expat workers, after one noticed their British Land Rover parked at Dhahran airport, such was the rarity of any foreign vehicles in the country at the time (and still, although a few European overlanders are trickling in from UAE!).

Flares in the desert: road from Riyadh to Dhahran

Getting there

Most people arrive here by air. There are good road links to Kuwait, Bahrain, the UAE and a new road direct to Oman.

Accommodation

As usual, check the major booking websites for options. Most will be quite pricey, with many oil men in town. This is Dallas on the Gulf!

Eating
Suffice to say that the choice will be international with so many guest workers from across the world.

Historical background
Little is known about the region in earlier times, except that the coast was inhabited by people surviving through pearl diving. Since the 1970s, the cities have grown incredibly.

The sights
If oil installations, ports and the lives of migrant workers are your passion, then there might be some interest here! Otherwise the towns merely act as overnight stopovers en route to the sights in the desert to the east, like Al Ahsa near Hofuf. The main sights are only outlined here, since we have not visited for the last 45 years! Sorry, more places to visit next time!

Al Ahsa
Close to Hofuf, the site is noted mainly for its desert outcrops. For some ideas about the type of rock formations and outcrops that exist here, check out 'Saudi desert rock outcrops and canyons' on Google. About 60km inland from the Arabian Gulf, it was once the main city in Al Bahrain Province. The unusual features are sculpted into the limestone layers with differing shades of white. Being close to the sea, it has plant life among the outcrops sustained by the humid moisture-laden skies of the Gulf that penetrate inland.

Flowers of the desert

Al Qarah Caves
Quite close to Hofuf are some notable caves and outcrops. The white coloured outcrops are quite different from those seen elsewhere and the remote nature of the area is striking.

Tarut & Al-Uqair

Tarut is an island on the Arabian Gulf, joined to Al-Qatif by a 4km natural land bridge. The historic town of Tarut on the island has a few archaeological sites, some of which date back to 5000–4000BC. Others have been linked to the Ilamite, Sassanian, Persian and perhaps the Mohenjodaro civilisation of ancient Pakistan. The pre-Islamic eastern port of Al-Uqair hosts old government buildings and a mosque dating to the King Abdul-Aziz era.

The Pipeline Road

This was the only transit road available to drivers seeking to reach the Gulf from Jordan years ago, including some expats. It ran from Amman into Saudi Arabia very close to the border with Iraq, through Turayf, Al Jalamid, Ratha and Ash Shu'bah to the Gulf coast. These days the area adjacent to Iraq is not deemed very safe due to the instability north of the border.

Al Wajh: Roundabout decorations, coffee time!

Highway across the An Nefud desert

The wild and rugged country of the Asir Highlands

Or the hurly-burly of modernity

Jeddah: Al Balad old city, famous for its doors and windows

The future for tourism? Golden Address Hotel outside Madinah

Sunset over the Red Sea

Sundown on Jeddah

The last word

Few visitors will initially come to Saudi Arabia for what is a 'normal' holiday, although beach-style vacations may well develop in the north close to Jordan and Sharm el Sheikh.

A trip to Saudi Arabia will, for most people, be chosen for its fascination and to gaze upon sights that have long been off-limits for tourism. Until recently it would have been considered a strange destination to visit for recreational purposes. Then again, many of the most amazing places in the world, like Chad or Somaliland, are not on the radar of most people. Sometimes such places are worth the extra mile of effort, and, dare we say it, an element of apprehension!

The reality of actually taking the plunge and booking a trip to Saudi Arabia at this stage in its tourist development will invariably be laced with much anticipation and probably some trepidation. How tourism will develop is anyone's guess. If you really want to go to the wild Arabia of your dreams, go now.

Have a safe and happy trip!

****

It's the beginning that's the worst, then the middle, then the end. But in the end, it's the end that's the worst.
Samuel Beckett

The door has creaked open on Saudi Arabia

APPENDICES

Appendix 1: Suggested trip schedules

Routes
Any trip to Saudi Arabia really needs a couple of weeks to do it justice and to have some down time. Even then it probably means a choice between the northern deserts or the southern highlands. Trying to fit in both areas can just about be done in 16 days, but it's not relaxing. To visit the capital and the eastern areas would need three weeks, and as for the Empty Quarter, maybe a lifetime if you are not prudent!

Most trips from Riyadh to the Empty Quarter take a week or so, but add in the remote and unknown sand seas of the southwest and it's going to be longer.

Taking public transport is time-consuming and also needs longer. Flights may be required to cut time. Getting to Al Ula by bus, for example, is long, as the route goes along the coast, then via Tabuk.

Option A: (17–20 days)
This is possible with a hired car. Even so it's a bit tight for the places mentioned below and not very relaxing. The trip below is our route in December, which was very rushed and depended on accommodation options as we found them – or not (none at Wadi Qaraqir and fully booked at Al Ula).

Day 1   Jeddah arrival
Day 2   Jeddah
Day 3   Madinah, outside the city
Day 4   Al Ula
Day 5   Al Ula/Mada'in Salih – ideally add a day
Day 6   Shigry via Wadi Qaraqir   +++ see below
Day 7   Tayma via Tabuk
Day 8   Khaybar
Day 9   Madinah via White Volcanoes
Day 10 Taif via Wabah Crater
Day 11 Al Bahah/Baljureshi/Ash Shaykh
Day 12 Abha – ideally add a day
Day 13 Qunfudhah via Rijal al-Ma
Day 14 East Jeddah via Makkah ring road
Day 15 Jeddah
Day 16 Spare day

+++ **Note:** Stay in Shwaq and add a day to explore Wadi Qaraqir. Even better, camp in the wadi or find somewhere to stay when possible.

Option B: (9–10 days)
With just over a week or so, it will be necessary to choose between the northern deserts or the southern mountains. The following is divided into two choices. These options also need a car.

North
Day 1   Jeddah arrival
Day 2   Jeddah
Day 3   Khaybar
Day 4   Al Ula
Day 5   Al Ula/Mada'in Salih
Day 6   Shigry via Wadi Qaraqir
Day 7   Tayma
Day 8   Khaybar/Al Thamad via White Volcanoes
Day 9   Jeddah via Madinah
Day 10 Spare day

South
Day 1   Jeddah
Day 2   Taif
Day 3   Al Bahah
Day 4   Baljureshi via Zee al-Ayn
Day 5   Abha
Day 6   Abha or Rijal al-Ma if hotel opens
Day 7   Qunfudhah via Rijal al-Ma
Day 8   Jeddah
Day 9   Spare day

Option C (8–9 days) Riyadh and the Empty Quarter
The following could be added to the above. Flights could be used between Jeddah and Riyadh, and another car hired. This trip is currently offered by local agents as a 3–4 day desert expedition.

Day 1   Riyadh arrival
Day 2   Riyadh, trip to Diriyah
Day 3   Drive to Wadi Ad-Dawasir and into the desert
Day 4   Desert dune area
Day 5   Desert and drive to Layla
Day 6   Drive to Riyadh
Day 7   Spare

Option D (8–10 days) Empty Quarter
Longer trips are being proposed from Riyadh to the Empty Quarter, but there is little information as yet. Hopefully Najran can be added at some stage in the future.

Any of the above can probably be organised by a travel agent when they are more familiar and experienced in organising tours and expeditions for overseas individuals and groups. These options are currently rather expensive.

Option E: (21–28 days)

This Grand Circle option takes in about as much as possible. Even so, a few sights might be missed without a massive detour, perhaps places like Al Wajh, Yanbu or Tayma.

Day 1   Ar Riyadh arrival
Day 2   Ar Riyadh
Day 3   Ar Riyadh, visit Diriyah
Day 4   Shaqra
Day 5   Buraydah via Ushaiger
Day 6   Ha'il via Fayd
Day 7   Dumat al-Jandal via Jubbah
Day 8   Dumat al-Jandal, Sakaka
Day 9   Tabuk
Day 10   Al Bada/Madyan via Jebel Hisma (a)
Day 11   Duba via Wells of Moses/Tayeb al-Ism (b)
Day 12   Wadi Qaraqir/Shigry (c)
Day 13   Spare
Day 14   Al Ula
Day 15   Al Ula, Mada'in Salih
Day 16   Al Ula, trip to Al Ragassan/Jibal al-Rukkab (d)
Day 17   Khaybar
Day 18   Khaybar, White and Black volcanoes
Day 19   Madinah
Day 20   Taif via Wabah Crater
Day 21   Baljureshi or Ranyah
Day 22   Abha or Wadi Ad Dawasir
Day 23   Abha, trip to Rijal al-Ma
Day 24   Najran via Wadi Ad Dawasir or Qal at Bishah from Abha (e)
Day 25   Sulayyil via Bir Hima, Al Faw or Uruq Bani Ma'arid res. (f)
Day 26   Layla
Day 27   Riyadh via Hawtat Bani Tamim oasis
Day 28   Riyadh

Notes:
(a)   Add a day in Jebel Hisma with a guide from Tabuk
(b)   Walking through the canyon Tayeb al-Ism add a day
(c)   Shaq canyon, add a day with guide/4X4
(d)   Extended trek, add a day or more and camp
(e)   If it's still necessary to avoid the road from Abha to Najran, go via Qal at Bishah
(f)   Add a day to overnight in Uruq Bani Ma'arid reserve; get a permit first

Appendix 2: Bibliography

Al Kamaan, Kamaan. **Roots of Saudi Heritage** Kamaan Al Kamaan

Al Obaida, Abdulaziz; Babelli, Mohammed; & Greenberg, Elizabeth. **Rub al-Khali: Empty Quarter**

Ansary, Abdul Rahman & Ḥusayn, Abu Al-Ḥassān. **The civilization of two cities: Al-Ula & Mada'in Sāliḥ,** Dar Al-Qawafil 2001

Al-Faqih, Kamal. **Classic Lebanese Cuisine: 170 Fresh and Healthy Mediterranean Favorites** Globe Pequot Press 2009

Babelli, Mohammed. **Visitors Guide to Mada'in Saleh**

Anderson, Norman. **The Kingdom of Saudi Arabia** Medina

Benson, Stephana V. **Birds of Lebanon and the Jordan Area** 1970

Blunt, Anne. **A Pilgrimage to Nejd** 1881 maybe reprints!

Bowen H, Wayne. **The History of Saudi Arabia** (second edition) Greenwood Histories series

Doughty, Charles M. **Arabia Deserta** 1888 Reprints

Faizer, R.; Ismail, A.; & Tayob, A. **The Life of Muhammad: al-Waqidi's Kitab al-Maghazi.** Routledge 2013

Healey, John. **The Nabatean Tomb Inscriptions of Mada'in Salih**

Hourani, Albert. **A History of the Arab peoples** Faber 1991

Lawrence T. E. **Seven Pillars of Wisdom** various

Murphy, David. **The Arab Revolt 1916–18** Bloomsbury

Nairn, A.E.M. & Alsharhan A.S. **Sedimentary Basins and Petroleum Geology of the Middle East**. Elsevier Science 1997

Olsen, Sandra. **Stories in the Rocks; exploring Saudi Arabian Rock Art** Carnegie 2013

Palgrave, William Gifford. **Narrative of a Year's Journey through Central and Eastern Arabia** Classic Reprints Forgotten Books 2012

Peters, F.E. **The Hajj: The Muslim pilgrimage to Mecca and the holy places**. Princeton University Press 1996

Pritchard-Jones, Sian & Gibbons, Bob. **A Brief Guide to Lebanon** Expedition World/Amazon 2019

Pritchard-Jones, Sian & Gibbons, Bob. **The Horn of Africa** Expedition World/Amazon 2016, 2020

Scott, Alev. **Ottoman Odyssey: Travels through a Lost Empire**, Riverrun Quercus Hachette UK 2018

Middle East Travel Guides, various countries Lonely Planet

Stillman, Norman. **The Jews of Arab Lands: A History and Source Book.** Philadelphia

Do you want to do a U-Turn?

Appendix 3: Glossary

Abbasids ruled across the Middle East from 750AD until the Mongol invasion of 1258AD

Ayyubids a dynasty who followed Saladin

Baksheesh commonly used word meaning 'tips'

Chalcolithic the period between the Neolithic and the Bronze age in the Middle East

Diwan carved-out recess with seats on three sides; audience hall

Fatimids Shia followers of Fatima, daughter of the Prophet Muhammad pbuh

Hajj the annual Muslim pilgrimage to Makkah/Mecca, beginning on the eighth and ending on the thirteenth day of Dhu al-Hijjah, the twelfth month of the Islamic calendar

Hijrah the migration of Muhammad pbuh and his followers from Makkah to Madinah in 622AD

Ihram the name given to the special spiritual state in which pilgrims wear two white sheets of seamless cloth and abstain from certain actions

Kaaba sacred stone at the centre of the mosque in Makkah

Khan or **Caravanserai** overnight stop on a long trade route

Madrassa religious school of Islam

Merlon 5-stepped triangle above tombs in Mada'in Salih

Mezze appetiser dishes, often filling, before a main course

Nahr river

Nabateans (Nabataeans) civilisation that ruled from Petra in Jordan with an outpost centred at Mada'in Salih

Omayyads or **Umayyads** dynasty who ruled from 661AD from Damascus until overthrown by the Abbasids in 750AD

Petroglyphs rock art where the surface has been etched

Qalat fort

Qasaba watch towers or granaries found in the southern hills

Qasr Fort, castle, could be a rock outcrop

Quran (Koran) the holy scriptures of Islam

Ramadan the 9th month of the Islamic calendar, the month when the Quran was completely revealed to the Prophet Muhammad (pbuh)

Seleucids came after Alexander the Great (312–64BC) and inherited his empire from Greece to India

Souk bazaar full of shops, often covered

Sufi mystical sect of Islam, characterised by dance, music and other liberal themes of the religion. Many consider Sufis to be heretics

Umrah pilgrimage to the holy sites outside the Hajj period

This may be useful finding a hotel!

Where is a hotel?	اين يوجد فندق

Appendix 4: Language hints

It's going to be a seriously big effort to learn enough words to hold a conversation, so here are a few helpful language hints:

Greetings	salaam aleikum
Greeting (in reply)	aleikum alsalaam
Good morning	sabah alkhyr
Good evening	masa' alkhyr
Please	raja'
Thank you	shukran
How are you	kayf halik
I am fine	ana bikhayr
Where is a hotel	ayn yujad funduq
What is your name?	ma aismak
Which way to *Al Ula*	aya tariq 'iilaa *Al Ula*
Hotel	funduq
Restaurant	mateam
How much is the cost	kam hi altakalifa
Peace be upon Him	salaa allah ealayh wasalam

Numbers:

Also useful are the numbers for road signs and currency bills:

1	١	wahid
2	٢	athnan
3	٣	thlath
4	٤	arbe
5	٥	khms
6	٦	st
7	٧	sbe
8	٨	thmany
9	٩	tise
10	١٠	eshr
11	١١	ahd eshr
20	٢٠	eshrwn
50	٥٠	khamsun
100	١٠٠	miaya
140	١٤٠	miat wa'arbaeun

Appendix 5: Useful contacts

Tour operators in Saudi Arabia
Inbound tourism is in its infancy. Try the following:
Al-Anazi, Mohammad mh3ww@yahoo.com
Amazing Tours www.amazingtours.com.sa
Arabian Camp www.arabiancamp.com
Horizon Tours www.thehorizonstours.com
Palm Land Tours www.pltksa.com

Tour operators overseas
Very few travel companies offer Saudi Arabia at this point.
Try the following:
Fliegel Jezerniczky Expeditions www.fjexpeditions.com
Oasis Overland www.oasisoverland.co.uk
Responsible Travel www.responsibletravel.co.uk
Steppes Travel www.steppestravel.com
Wild Frontiers www.wildfrontierstravel.com

Visa agencies
Travcour (London) www.travcour.com
Fast Visas (Paris) www.fastvisa.fr

Online information
www.expeditionworld.com (travel site run by the authors)
www.fco.gov.uk/travel – UK travel advice and tips
www.diplomatie.gouv.fr – French government website
www.viaggiaresicuri.it – Italian government website

www.stanfords.co.uk – maps
www.themapshop.co.uk – maps
www.themapcentre.com – maps
www.trekkingpartners.com – to find a trekking partner

www.againstthecompass.com (Joan)
www.blueabaya.com (Laura)
www.onthewayaround.com/saudi-arabia-travel-guide (Jacob)
www.susieofarabia.blogspot.com (Susie)
www.susiesbigadventure.blogspot.com (Susie)
www.saudiarabiatourismguide.com (Florent)
www.lonelyplanet.com/thorntree/forums/middle-east/saudi-arabia

www.britannica.co.uk – Encyclopaedia Britannica
www.medomed.org
www.researchgate.net
www.sauditourism.sa
www.saudia-archeology.com
www.saudicaves.com
www.theislamicinformation.com
whc.unesco.org/en/list/1293/
www.volcanodiscovery.com

About the authors

Authors windswept at Wabah Crater

Siân Pritchard-Jones and Bob Gibbons met in 1983, on a trek from Kashmir to Ladakh. By then Bob had already driven an ancient Land Rover from England to Kathmandu (in 1974), and overland trucks across Asia, Africa and South America. He had also lived in Kathmandu for two years, employed as a trekking company manager. Before they met, Siân worked in computer programming and systems analysis. Since they met they have been leading and organising treks in the Alps, Nepal and the Sahara, as well as driving a bus overland to Nepal. Journeys by a less ancient (only 31-year-old) Land Rover from England to South Africa provided the basis for several editions of the Bradt guide **Africa Overland**, including the sixth edition published in April 2014.

In 2007 they wrote the Cicerone guide to **Mount Kailash** and Western Tibet, as well updating the **Grand Canyon** guide. Their **Annapurna** trekking guide was first published by Cicerone in January 2013, with the 2nd edition in 2017. They were in Nepal during the 2015 earthquakes and published **Earthquake Diaries: Nepal 2015**.

A Pictorial Guide to the **Horn of Africa** (Djibouti, Eritrea, Ethiopia and Somaliland), **Australia: Red Centre Treks** and **In Search of the Green-Eyed Yellow Idol**, a 40-year travelogue & autobiography, are all published by Expedition World/CreateSpace/Kindle/Amazon.

Kanchi's Tale covers various expeditions as seen through the eyes of a Nepalese mountain dog – an educational doggie travelogue!

For Himalayan Map House they are writing a new series of trekking guidebooks: **Himalayan Travel Guides**. See next page for titles so far published. All books are also available on Amazon websites worldwide.

Other books by the authors

Bradt (www.bradtguides.com)
Africa Overland --- 2005, 2009, 2014 new edition due 2021

Cicerone (www.cicerone.co.uk)
The Mount Kailash Trek --- 2007
Annapurna: A Trekker's Guide --- 2013, 2016

Amazon / Kindle (www.amazon.com)
In Search of the Green-Eyed Yellow Idol --- 2015, 2019
(an autobiography)
Earthquake Diaries: Nepal 2015 --- 2015
The Horn of Africa: A Pictorial Guide --- 2016, 2020
Australia: Red Centre Treks --- 2016
Kanchi's Tale: Kanchi goes to Makalu Base Camp --- 2017
Kanchi goes to the Tibesti, Chad --- 2017
Chad: Tibesti, Ennedi & Borkou --- 2017, 2020
Karakoram: The Highway of History --- 2018
Ladakh: A Land of Mystical Monasteries --- 2018
Lebanon: A Brief Guide --- 2019
Karakoram & K2 Concordia (trekking guide) --- 2019
Saudi Arabia: A Traveller's Guide --- 2020
Saudi Arabia: A Pictorial Guide --- 2020
South America: A Pictorial Guide --- 2020
Africa Overland: A Pictorial Guide --- 2020
Asia Overland: A Pictorial Guide --- 2020
Tibet: A Pictorial Guide --- 2020
Nepal Himalaya: A Pictorial Guide --- 2020
Kathmandu: Valley of the Green-Eyed Yellow Idol --- 2020

Himalayan Map House HMH (www.himalayanmaphouse.com)
Himalayan Travel Guides HTG (www.himalayantravelguides.com)
& Amazon worldwide (www.amazon.com)
Manaslu & Tsum Valley --- 2013, 2016, 2019, 2020
Dolpo --- 2014, 2019, 2020; Ganesh Himal --- 2014
Langtang --- 2014, 2018, 2020; Everest --- 2014, 2018
Rolwaling --- 2015; Mustang --- 2016, 2019, 2020
Kanchenjunga --- 2017; Makalu --- 2017, 2020
West Nepal --- 2017; Dhaulagiri --- 2018
Nepal Himalaya --- 2015, 2017, 2019

Pilgrims (www.pilgrimsonlineshop.com)
Kathmandu: Valley of the Green-Eyed Yellow Idol --- 2005
Ladakh: Land of Magical Monasteries --- 2006
Kailash & Guge: Land of the Tantric Mountain --- 2006

Answer: the photo on page 232 was taken at the Crabe d'Arakao, Ténéré, Niger. Sadly it is currently unsafe to visit.

Index

Printed in Great Britain
by Amazon

52591350R00149